Find Strength Through Crisis

TIME
LIFE
BOOKS

MINDPOWER
JOURNEY THROUGH THE MIND AND BODY
COOKERY AROUND THE WORLD
LOST CIVILIZATIONS
THE ILLUSTRATED LIBRARY OF THE EARTH
SYSTEM EARTH
LIBRARY OF CURIOUS AND UNUSUAL FACTS
BUILDING BLOCKS
A CHILD'S FIRST LIBRARY OF LEARNING
VOYAGE THROUGH THE UNIVERSE
THE THIRD REICH
MYSTERIES OF THE UNKNOWN
TIME-LIFE HISTORY OF THE WORLD
FITNESS, HEALTH & NUTRITION
HEALTHY HOME COOKING
UNDERSTANDING COMPUTERS
THE ENCHANTED WORLD
LIBRARY OF NATIONS
PLANET EARTH
THE GOOD COOK
THE WORLD'S WILD PLACES

MINDPOWER

Find Strength Through Crisis

TIME-LIFE BOOKS
Amsterdam

MINDPOWER

Created, edited, and designed by DK Direct Limited,
62-65 Chandos Place, London WC2N 4HS

A DORLING KINDERSLEY BOOK

DK DIRECT LIMITED
Series Editor Luci Collings
Deputy Series Editor Sue Leonard
Senior Editor Christine Murdock
Editors Claire Calman, Tean Mitchell
Managing Art Editor Ruth Shane
Art Editor Sarah Mulligan
Designer Luke Herriott

Publisher Jonathan Reed
Editorial Director Reg Grant
Design Director Tony Foo
Production Manager Ian Paton

Editorial Consultants Keren Smedley and Denis Sartain
Contributors Vida Adamoli, Sheila Cane,
Victoria Davenport, Sue George, Sarah Halliwell,
Ann Kay, Christine Murdock, Ruth Shane

Editorial Researcher L. Brooke
Indexer Ella Skene

TIME-LIFE BOOKS EUROPEAN EDITION
Staff for Find Strength Through Crisis
Editorial Manager Christine Noble
Editorial Assistant Mark Stephenson
Design Director Mary Staples
Designer Dawn McGinn
Editorial Production Justina Cox
European edition edited by Tim Cooke

First Time-Life European English language edition 1996
ISBN 0 7054 1635 6
TIME-LIFE is a trademark of Time-Warner Inc., U.S.A.

Printed by GEA, Milan, and bound by GEP, Cremona, Italy

30 29 28 27 26 25 24 23 22 21 20 19 18 17 16 15 14 13 12 11 10 9 8 7 6 5 4 3 2 1

CONTENTS

INTRODUCTION

THE VERY MENTION OF THE WORD CRISIS might be enough to make your heart beat faster, conjuring up an image of a personal tragedy, such as a divorce or a terrible illness: some event striking out of the blue, undermining the very core of your life, security, and happiness. In fact, the dictionary defines crisis as a "turning point or time of decision, an unstable or crucial time where there is an impending decisive change." The Chinese written symbol, or pictogram, for crisis combines two characters—one meaning danger and one meaning opportunity—expressing the idea that a crisis also carries with it the potential for progress or new growth.

Some events almost inevitably result in a crisis: war, for example, and disasters such as plane crashes, fires, sieges, and traumatic personal assaults. Other situations may generate insecurity but need not be crises; for example, when children grow up and leave home, parents have to refocus on their partnership and their own lives. The changes this involves—the sense of loss, the reassessment of a long-established relationship—may precipitate a crisis such as an affair or marital breakdown. By contrast, some couples discover that fewer responsibilities and more free time is very liberating. In all cases, the extent to which a situation becomes a crisis depends significantly on an individual's personality, emotional history, behavior, and responses, as well as on the responses of the people around them.

In general, a crisis is a process and a transition rather than a single, fixed event. It is an opportunity for you to develop and learn—even if it also initiates a period when you turn inward and withdraw from the world. The least effective response is to deny that there is a problem in need of resolution.

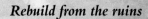

Rebuild from the ruins
A crisis may seem like a catastrophe, but it can help you "clear the decks," providing a rare opportunity to make a fresh start.

TURNING POINTS

Throughout our lives, we must all confront and live through a series of crises related to each stage of our natural growth and development. Some of these situations apply to all of us, such as coping with the physical changes and emotional confusion of puberty; others, such as getting divorced or coping with an emotionally disturbed family member, may never happen to you, but are very common.

How we cope with these life changes depends on whether or not we have a supportive social context as well as on our personalities and the specific circumstances of the crisis. How society in general and a family in particular view old age, for example, affects not only an older person's own view, but also how involved and socially integrated he or she remains. Elderly people who become isolated are less likely to cope well with ageing. In societies where the elderly are appreciated and respected for their greater experience and wisdom, old age is less likely to be a time to be feared or to provoke a crisis.

Know your breaking point

Do you know what your breaking point is? One person might be able to tolerate a high level of prolonged stress yet still be able to cope well when an emergency arises. For someone else already under a great deal of pressure, however, having the car break down or the electricity fail could be the catalyst that triggers a crisis.

For all you know, a major change could be lying just around the corner. How you react and how you will cope will be influenced by your personal history, but the pressure may be eased if you can anticipate stressful turning points. Certain transitions, such as marriage or the impending birth of a first child, are ones you can prepare for. *Find Strength Through Crisis* will help you anticipate potential crisis areas in your life, become more aware of how you react in a crisis, and use the challenges and difficulties you face in life to develop your inner resources and gain strength and wisdom.

A time for change

Whenever a crisis occurs, it is usually both the result of change, and the impetus for future change. Sometimes, an event is forced upon you, and you have no choice but to respond and cope—a sudden death, illness, or even a happy event such as a windfall or a promotion. A sudden change often demands immediate action. Many people describe switching to "automatic pilot" during a crisis, even a positive one. The shock waves rippling out from these events may lead to a series of smaller crises as we try to adapt to the new situation. Many people prefer to stick with what is familiar because it makes them feel safe and comfortable. Any change will challenge your security and established ways of thinking and behaving: By implication, change of any kind can feel very threatening, a cause of deep anxiety and insecurity as people feel it may disrupt all aspects of their lives, not just the area first affected.

Congratulations—crisis ahead!

You might not think of good news and events as creating a problem, but many apparently positive situations can trigger a crisis. Part of the difficulty is that people feel pressured to be happy about their good fortune—particularly if it is something you have been looking forward to for some time—when, in fact, you may feel anxious, depressed, scared, and unable to cope. For example, when two people get married they may find the

Looking ahead
As you work through a crisis, you can look ahead to the future and start planning the positive changes you can make by using the wisdom and strength you have gained from your experience.

demands of living together and sharing their time, space, and lives very difficult; it may feel like a threat to their individuality and independence. The birth of a baby, with all the implied extra responsibilities, work, and possible mixed emotions, can also lead to a period of confusion, self-doubt, fear, and even panic.

Equipped for survival

How well you can cope in a crisis will be determined by many factors, including your current physical, mental, and emotional state, how your parents dealt with change and crises, your self-esteem, and your fundamental views about yourself and your life. Identifying your personal strengths and possible areas of weakness will give you insight into the way you tackle crises. It will also help you determine what changes you could make to improve the way you act and respond to future crises; you may then be able to defuse potentially explosive problems and handle times of stress before they have a chance to develop into full-blown crises. Learning how to help yourself, and how to turn to others for help and support when you need it, will consolidate your own strength. This will, in turn, enable you to marshal all your available resources. Your strength will carry you safely through crises to the opportunities for change and growth that lie beyond.

STRESS AND CRISIS

Not every problematic situation is a crisis. Sometimes, however, long-term stress, or a sudden increase in stress, can make it feel as though you are living through a crisis. It is important to distinguish between what is simply a stressful situation and what is a crisis because the difference affects how you manage your responses. Also, if you realize that you are undergoing a transitional period with the potential for change, it can make it easier to endure the difficult times. The factors below are key characteristics of crises:

• A trigger event has occurred, such as a sudden loss or significant change.
• There has been stress over a long period of time.
• There is a feeling of loss, danger, and sometimes humiliation.
• The situation feels outside your control.
• The event feels unexpected, although it may well have been signposted earlier or built up over time.
• There has been a fairly drastic interruption of everyday life and routine.
• The anxiety and distress continues over a period of two to eight weeks.
• There is a risk of the situation becoming worse. You may fear that you will be unable to cope.
• There is potential for future change.

The end of the world?
In the middle of a crisis, you may feel as if your whole world is collapsing around you, undermining your sense of security and leaving you with no hope of recovery.

Are you aware of potential crisis areas in your life? Answer the following questions, divided into categories of the kinds of crises that often occur. If you answer "yes" to a question, it doesn't mean that you are in a crisis, or will have one soon. You should be alert for signs of future difficulties, however, and refer to the relevant pages in this book.

1. Age
• *Are you 35-55? Or 65 or over?*
Midlife is a dangerous time for possible depression. In an attempt to keep these feelings at bay, men and women may abandon long-standing relationships. Mood swings are normal (see pp. 24-27).

In later years, people may have a less reliable memory and physical changes such as decreasing suppleness and stamina or, more seriously, declining health. The awareness of these changes, as well as the changes themselves, can be very distressing (see pp. 28-29).

2. Relationships
• *Are you having relationship problems?*
• *Did you recently marry or start living with a partner?*
• *Have you recently become single or widowed?*
Any major change in a close relationship may lead to a crisis. Even positive changes, such as marriage and pregnancy, may trigger intense anxiety (see pp. 64-67). Becoming single again after being in a relationship can be painful and damage your self-esteem and confidence (see pp. 38-39). The death or loss of a partner rates high on stress-assessment charts (see pp. 50-53).

3. Career
• *Have you been fired or made redundant in the last year?*
• *Have you recently been promoted or started a new job?*
• *Have you been unemployed for more than a year?*
• *Will you retire soon, or have you retired in the last year?*
Although we rarely think of positive events, such as a promotion or retirement, as crises, they can be frightening. Losing your job can be a major source of depression, as can long-term unemployment (see pp. 42-43). Surprisingly, pursuing a long-held dream of self-employment can be quite stressful. Voluntary or involuntary retirement, often occurring when people are worried about being "past their prime," can also exacerbate feelings of uselessness and loss of identity (see pp. 74-75).

4. Physical health
• *Have you suffered any kind of serious illness in the last six months?*
• *Do you have symptoms of severe stress, such as headaches, sleeping problems, repeated colds or flu, skin disorders, etc.?*
• *Is someone close to you seriously ill?*
• *Have you had to devote much time and energy to caring for someone else in the last year?*
Serious or long-term illness can wreak havoc on your emotional life as well as on your physical well-being. People are often surprised that the shock waves of a heart attack or major surgery can go on for months afterward (see pp. 46-47). If you have a chronic illness, you may be headed for a crisis. Similarly, if you are close to someone who is ill, you may become involved in their crisis (see pp. 46-47), especially if you have been coping on your own and have felt reluctant to ask others for help.

5. Death and loss
• *Has someone close to you—a family member or friend—died within the last six to 12 months?*
• *Is someone close to you terminally ill?*
• *Has a very close friend moved away or got married?*
• *Have you recently separated from a partner?*
The death or loss of someone close is a major source of stress and emotional turmoil. It can trigger memories of earlier losses and precipitate a crisis that may continue for months or years (see pp. 50-53). Grief and loss arouse unexpected feelings, including anger and guilt as well as sadness and depression.

6. Criminal assault

• *Have you ever been raped, or sexually assaulted or abused?*

• *Have you ever been physically assaulted or abused?*

• *Have you been burgled or robbed in the last year?*

The violation of your body, belongings, or space can have a devastating effect on your sense of yourself and the world around you. As well as any physical hurt, the emotional and psychological ramifications can be long-lasting. In cases of personal assault or abuse, expert help and support may be vital in enabling the victim to work through the pain and fear (see pp. 54-57).

7. Parenthood

• *Have you had your first child in the last year?*

The nine months before the birth of a child are not enough to prepare people for the dramatic—and permanent—changes about to take place. New parents may feel both joy and panic, overwhelmed by the many practical demands of looking after a young baby (see pp. 66-67).

8. Moving house

• *Have you moved house, or taken a long trip to a foreign country, in the last year?*

Any major change of environment may touch on our need for safety, familiarity, and protection. When we are in a new place or setting, we tend to be more anxious and watchful, less secure in our behavior and our sense of our own identity; for some people, this can lead to a crisis (see pp. 68-69).

9. Good news!

• *Have you won any big prizes in the last six months?*

• *Have you inherited a large sum of money or a property from a relative or friend?*

Good news may bring many benefits, but it can also herald bad news in terms of the changes it may cause in your life and your family. For example, inheriting money can lead to resentment, envy, and family in-fighting, and even guilt because it is associated with grief and loss. Even winning a lottery can create a crisis that people may find hard to negotiate. Additional pressure comes from the fact that you are expected to be over the moon, even if you are actually feeling panicky and confused (see pp. 76-77).

10. Multiple changes

• *Have you experienced more than one of the above events in the last six to 12 months?*

Experiencing more than one significant event in a short period—for example, getting married, moving house, and having a baby, or suffering a bereavement and getting promoted—may overload you with stress and catapult you into a state of crisis (see pp. 80-81). The intensity of this will depend on the particular combination of events and on your emotional and physical state. If you feel overwhelmed by a number of life changes, it is important that you take steps to seek support; counseling or psychotherapy may help (see pp. 132-135).

Handle with care

No-one can cope with excessive stress over a long period. Too many major changes in your life can endanger your sense of security and stability and cause a serious crisis.

CHECK YOUR CRISIS RESPONSE

How do you react in a crisis? Are you anxious that you might not be able to cope? Or do you tend to block out painful feelings and try to carry on as normal? How you react in a crisis is determined by your current mental, emotional, and physical health, and by your personality, experience, and support network. If any of these elements is unstable or under threat, you are more likely to respond in an extreme or counterproductive way. For example, if your health is poor and you are then put under great stress, you might suffer further ill health.

Helpful or unhelpful?

Responses to crises cover a wide spectrum, ranging from psychosomatic reactions such as skin problems or sleepiness to hyperactivity or intense grief. While there is no single "correct" response to a crisis, some reactions are more positive and emotionally healthy than others. The following examples illustrate how three different people responded to the death of a parent.

Mixed emotions: When Barbara's mother died after a long illness, Barbara felt both deep sadness and relief. At times, she felt calm and peaceful, but at other times she felt very distressed and guilty, wondering if she could have done more to help.

Barbara was able to acknowledge the relief she felt. This can be very difficult to do since it may seem wrong to feel relieved when someone dies, but it is understandable if a person has been in pain or ill for a long time. Her deep sadness and guilt are also part of a predictable response to grief. Bereaved people often have mood swings, which may be quite extreme and frightening, but are a normal response to many types of crisis (see "Death and Mourning," pp. 50-51, and "Stages of Grief," pp. 52-53).

Suppressed feelings: Sam heard the news of his father's death while at work. He had close friends and colleagues around at the time, but said nothing. Instead, he went back to his desk and worked. Sam

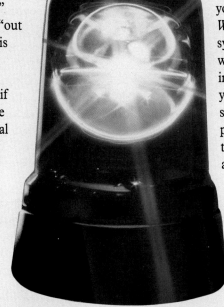

WARNING SIGNS

Each of us has our own way of thinking, feeling, and behaving, so it is hard to define what is a typical or "normal" reaction to a crisis. You might act "out of character" in a crisis, without this necessarily indicating a worrying problem. However, the following guidelines can help you determine if your reactions, or those of someone you are concerned about, are typical or a possible cause for worry.

Physical symptoms
Typical: You may temporarily experience anxiety, breathlessness, palpitations, sleeplessness, and loss of appetite. You may need to urinate frequently, and may also suffer diarrhea or constipation, colitis or stomach problems, skin disorders such as eczema and/or asthma, or dizziness or vertigo. Any chronic disorder you already suffer from may worsen.
Worrying: Contact your doctor if any symptom lasts longer than about eight weeks after the crisis has passed. Stress intensifies certain physical reactions; if you already have a serious condition such as heart trouble or high blood pressure, you should see your doctor at the first sign of warning symptoms such as severe chest pain or breathlessness.

Mental symptoms
Typical: During a crisis, you may feel confused, indecisive, or unable to concentrate, so you should try to postpone making major decisions.
Worrying: An overwhelming or prolonged crisis may result in

was probably deeply shocked when he heard of his father's death. The fact that he showed no emotion with his friends suggests that he might not turn to others in times of need or express his feelings. By bottling up his feelings, he risks illness or severe depression. If Sam continued to feel numb or blank for months afterward, he might be suffering from post-traumatic stress (see pp. 60-61).

Life's rough knocks
When caught in a crisis,
you may feel buffeted
by mood swings,
and entirely at
the mercy of
your emotions.

In flight: A week after her mother's sudden death, Lucy resigned from work, sold her flat, and bought a one-way ticket to a country where she knew absolutely no-one.

Lucy's reaction—running away from the crisis—is a very common one: The temptation to react to loss by changing our lives drastically is an attempt to deal with an overwhelming situation, but the consequences are rarely helpful. Although, in the short term, it may be more difficult to face a painful situation, in the long term it is more beneficial.

obsessional thinking (when you can't stop thinking or worrying about something), phobias, compulsive behavior (such as repeated checking or hand-washing), nightmares, irrational fears, and auditory or visual hallucinations.

Emotional symptoms

Typical: You may feel extreme grief, rage, or anxiety; sometimes your moods may swing drastically and unpredictably. Such feelings may last for a few weeks after the crisis, but then gradually become less severe.
Worrying: Numbness or detachment may signal an attempt to deny that a crisis has occurred. If you feel numb or depressed for more than a few days after the crisis, talk to your doctor or a counselor. Sometimes, in extreme cases, a person may feel desperate and suicidal. If you are worried about yourself or someone else, telephone an emergency support service or your doctor. Never feel ashamed to ask for help.

Take note

If you recognize any of the following signs of potentially serious problems in yourself or someone you know, you should seek professional help.
• Prolonged withdrawal from family and friends
• Numbness and a feeling of detachment or unreality
• Deep depression and despair
• Suicidal thoughts
• Feelings of not being able to cope
• Feelings of being out of control
• Fear of going mad, hallucinations, or hearing voices
• Obsessional thinking
• Feelings of being "got at" all the time
• Complete loss of sense of humor, pleasure, and fun
• Inability to express feelings
• Feelings of hopelessness and of being trapped
• Having minor accidents
• Feelings of an unbearable tension that never ceases
• Endless exhaustion.

CHAPTER ONE

TURNING POINTS

FROM TIME TO TIME, life inevitably involves crises. Some of them are simply part of the way we change and develop as we progress through life, which is why this opening chapter looks at transitions and periods of adjustment common to all of us. Understanding the possible implications of these changes, and being prepared for them, can help you integrate them into your life. You may then "rise to the occasion" more easily and gracefully, rather than feeling victimized by forces beyond your control.

"Rites of Passage," pages 16-17, pinpoints key phases and changes, such as puberty, marriage, midlife, and retirement. Acknowledging and celebrating these stages, rather than trying to ignore them or play down their importance, will help you to face significant changes with an optimistic frame of mind.

Childhood (pp. 18-19) is a time of learning and discovery, but also of confusion and frustration as a child struggles with new knowledge and skills, and the demands of the world beyond the family. Adolescence (pp. 20-21) can be a particularly difficult and unhappy period. It is a stage when youngsters, who are neither children nor adults, struggle to define their identity, their changing bodies, and

a growing awareness of their sexuality. Because this phase is as confusing for parents as it is for adolescents, it frequently triggers intense family conflicts.

"Adulthood," pages 22-23, looks at the changes we initiate that may create great happiness but also unforeseen difficulties. Getting married or living with someone, for example, involves great upheaval, and means we have to learn the delicate art of negotiation. Starting work or having a baby are important, often happy, changes that demand flexibility and commitment.

Midlife—another critical transitional period, and commonly reputed to be a "crisis"—is discussed on pages 24-27. It is when we re-evaluate our lives, assess what we have done so far, and plan our futures. Retirement and the later years (see pp. 28-29) can be a difficult stage for many people, especially if their sense of identity has always been strongly rooted in how they earn their living. This may also be a time of painful loss, perhaps of a lifelong partner or close friends, or of your health. More positively, an awareness of our fragility and mortality can make us deeply appreciative of those we love, of the world around us, of our own talents and strengths—and of the time we have in which to enjoy them.

AS WE PARTICIPATE IN THE CYCLE OF LIFE AND GROW TO MATURITY,

WE PASS THROUGH DIFFERENT STAGES DURING WHICH

WE LEARN NEW LESSONS.

RITES OF PASSAGE

FROM THE CRADLE to the grave, we all go through key changes in our lives. Although these may vary in intensity from person to person, each significant life transition has certain characteristics—and each is a potential crisis point. Certain changes, such as puberty, occur gradually, and may therefore bring a number of changes in their wake, and, in some cases, more than one crisis. Others, such as marriage or retirement, may be marked by a single occasion, but the effects of the change persist long after the event.

All over the world, in societies and cultures that range from small, agricultural communities to large, industrial economies, people mark and celebrate life stages and important changes in various ways. Often, there are official ceremonies or organized rituals with long histories, although sometimes the significance of these changes is acknowledged by a party or more informal gathering.

Birth: A birth is usually a joyous event, and people in most cultures perform some kind of ceremony to welcome a new life into the world and to mark the infant's acceptance by the wider community. The ceremony also signals to this community that a couple are now parents and may need both practical and emotional support. The event may be religious and formal, such as a baptism, or popular and traditional, such as the Scottish custom of "wetting the baby's head," which sounds like a baptism but actually means having a drink to wish the infant good health.

Puberty: The start of sexual maturation can be a time of confusion and embarrassment for young people. In many, usually non-Western cultures, however, it is seen as a time for public rejoicing; for example, the onset of menstruation in girls may be celebrated rather than discussed in hushed tones. The Jewish bar mitzvah (for boys) and bat mitzvah (for girls) around the age of 13 marks the acceptance of religious duties and responsibilities, and, as such, is regarded as an important step toward adulthood.

Coming of age: This may involve several landmarks at different ages, such as passing the age of consent (being able legally to have sexual intercourse), being old enough to have a driving licence, and being eligible to vote, all signs of being an adult. Some people mark these occasions by having a party on, say, their 16th or 18th birthday. In the past, people in the United Kingdom were given the "key of the door" when they came of age—symbolizing their family's acceptance of them as adults. The custom of young, upper-class women, or debutantes, having a "coming out" ball for their formal entrance into society also signaled that they were now available for marriage.

Graduation: Having a ceremony to celebrate graduating from school or college recognizes the individual's hard work and achievement within the context of his or her peer group, and gives a student's family the chance to express their pride and joy at this achievement. These ceremonies usually have much greater significance than "end-of-term" observances because the time spent in academic work has been much longer, and the risk of success or failure is of far greater consequence. This turning point usually demands a serious re-evaluation of skills, talents, and goals, particularly when a person completes a university course or a post-graduate degree, and must make a decision about career goals.

Marriage: Usually rooted in long-standing customs, marriages may be religious or civil ceremonies, or traditional rituals such as the old Scottish "handfast" in which a betrothed couple take each other's hands in front of witnesses.

A public ceremony serves many important functions. Primarily a legal contract, marriage creates a socially sanctioned framework for raising children. It allows a couple to make a public commitment to each other and to their future life, and signals to the wider society that the two people are now a couple, and no longer available to other partners. A ceremony also enlists the support of members of the community, who, by giving gifts or money, help the couple to set up home.

Midlife: For many people, the age of 40 is a key turning point, a critical time to reassess their lives and consider their futures. Although there may not be an official ceremony to mark midlife, many people throw a 40th birthday party in recognition of its significance and as a way of celebrating the opportunities and life they still have to enjoy. For many, the phrase "Life begins at 40" is true.

Retirement: This can be a major life change, particularly for those who have worked all their lives. Many people fear the loss of self-worth, especially if their identity has been derived from what they *do* rather than who they *are,* or if they have always worked for one company. A retirement party is a way of congratulating someone on a productive working life, and marking an exciting, new chapter of his or her life.

Death: The rituals and customs surrounding death vary widely from culture to culture, but all make the committal of the body, usually by burial or cremation, part of a ceremony. Having a formal structure to frame an event that often involves great sadness and distress appears to be cathartic for most people. In many societies, a party is held to celebrate the life of the person—not to deny that death has occurred, but to recall the happiness the mourners shared with the deceased while he or she was alive.

Rituals stabilize life

Why do people all over the world find it necessary to adopt such rituals that may not seem to have much practical purpose? The obvious significance of all of these rituals is that they serve to connect the individual to the larger group to which he or she belongs: an extended family, a religious or ethnic group, a municipal community or a country.

Rituals also contribute to the psychological significance of an event for the participants. Some life events can threaten to overwhelm us, either because of the changes we feel will be thrust upon us, or because we think we will lose control of our feelings. The public recognition of life transitions, and the use of ceremonies to acknowledge their importance, helps you to integrate changes into your life at a slower pace, rather than feeling at the mercy of an unsought change. This is partly because they signal to those around you that you are in a period of change, and that they may need to make allowances for this or assist you. Rituals can help you harness and contain the potential for change, helping you grow and develop so that you can make the most of each phase of your life.

Signaling change
Marking key life changes or stages helps those around you recognize how important they are for you.

CHILDHOOD

CHILDHOOD is idealized as a time of happy innocence, free from the worries, dramas, and responsibilities of adult life. Essentially a period of development and learning—physical, mental, psychological, and social—it is a time of great discovery about the world around us, about other people, and about ourselves.

What is easily forgotten, however, is that it is also a time of confusion, insecurity, and frustration. If parents or carers handle such problems well, they can help the child to establish a stable emotional and psychological foundation, and to develop the capacity to handle problems rather than withdraw from them or magnify them into crises. As children mature, they grow intellectually, emotionally, and morally, and every strength they gain will be applied to the crises they will inevitably face.

The learning process

The world of the infant is often one of frustration, anger, and fear. A baby is entirely dependent on others yet unable to express its needs or feelings until it starts learning to communicate, first with cries and sounds, then with gestures and words. As the child grows up, the learning process continues, bringing inevitable setbacks and frustrations as well as successes. An obvious example is learning how to walk: Before discovering how to maintain his or her balance, a child will inevitably fall down.

A new arrival

When a second baby is born into a family, it is an incredible affront to its older sibling, who is suddenly knocked from his or her position as the parents' sole pride and joy. This can become a crisis as the child confronts the painful reality that his or her parents must be shared with someone else. Obviously displaced, he or she jealously and sometimes angrily witnesses the influx of family and friends who gush over the new baby. The trauma can be minimized, however, if the parents are aware of how the arrival of the baby might affect the older child, and continue to treat him or her with affection, patience, and encouragement.

Off to school

Children may feel abandoned when they first go to school, fearing that the parents will never come back. Parents should be reassuring without prolonging their good-byes, which only makes the temporary separation more significant. It helps to give children a toy from home to carry so that they have a familiar, comforting object.

Boundaries of love

Children go through a phase of feeling jealous of the same-sex parent. At this time, parents need to be seen to be united and to show their strong bond with each other, as well as express their love for the child. This helps the child realize that he or she cannot have the desired parent, is not more powerful than the parents, and will always be outside their special relationship with each other. Although painful, the sense of hurt can be borne more easily if the child feels secure in the love of both his or her parents.

Stages of growth
Childhood is a period of major physical, mental, and emotional growth; the changes that children face can seem daunting but, with help, they can find a way to accept and cope with them.

CHILDREN UNDER STRESS

Children often find it very hard to communicate feelings of hurt, insecurity, fear, anger, or anguish to their parents, partly because they may not have the words to explain how they feel, but also because they may be afraid of being teased, scolded, or ridiculed. There are often signs, however, such as obvious changes in behavior, that may indicate when a child is under stress. Warning signs to look for include the following:

• **Eating problems**, particularly not eating or becoming an anxious, "picky" eater. Don't be disturbed if your child has strong likes and dislikes, but do be concerned if he or she appears unhappy or morose, and consistently rejects all types of food—especially favorite foods or "treats."

• **Bedwetting** or soiling. If this occurs repeatedly once a child has been toilet-trained, it can be a way of expressing fear or anger. If it persists, you might want to consult your family doctor.

• **Nightmares**, fear of the dark. The child needs to be comforted and reassured that he or she is safe. It is helpful to encourage the child to talk about the nightmare at the time, and to see if it relates to any events going on in his or her life. A safe night light or landing light could be left on.

• **School problems**, particularly lack of friends, or school phobia (perhaps due to fear of bullying, punishment, or failure). Bullying in particular can be a very serious problem, and may be indicated by a child's extreme reluctance to go to school or by repeated claims of sickness with no obvious cause. Children should be encouraged to talk about their fears and the issue discussed with a sympathetic teacher.

• **Physical complaints.** If your child is not ill, complaints may indicate emotional problems, or, in a few serious cases, psychological or sexual abuse. Any illness can be used as a way of signaling that help is needed, either for the child or the parents.

• **Tantrums.** While difficult for parents to handle, tantrums are also frightening for the child, who fears that he or she is losing control. Rather than getting angry, the best response is to comfort the child, holding him or her firmly until the child calms down. Only when the tantrum has passed should you try to discuss the problem.

ADOLESCENCE

THIS IS A TIME of intense change. You may recall the exciting discoveries you made about the opposite sex, and about yourself and your talents and interests. For many people, however, their adolescence is also remembered as a time of confusion and deep hurt, of struggles with parents for greater freedom, for example, of anger and frustration when attempts at self-expression were met with disapproval. You may remember your injured pride when you were rejected by someone you had feelings for, or your worries about trying to "fit in" with your peers.

Adolescence is an awkward, transitional time, when boys and girls are no longer children but not yet adults either. In some ways, they may desire to remain children, to be able to return to a time of unencumbered "innocence," but they also want to be seen—and often demand to be treated—as "grown up," sophisticated, and independent.

Rebel with a cause

Although adolescents may conform to rigid rules established by their peers, they often rebel fiercely against parents, who are *also* confused and bewildered by this difficult, "in-between" phase. You may despair and feel that you have lost your cheerful and well-mannered child for ever, but your son or daughter with the strange hair and outlandish clothes may also feel lost, uncertain, and bereft.

While many good and creative things emerge from your child's struggle for independence, it is still a painful separation for you both. Your adolescent still needs your steadying hand for support and encouragement: Even if he or she fights you fiercely and loudly, your opinion *does* matter. Remember, too, that, as the adult, *you* may have to show maturity by being more flexible in your views.

Your changing child
Adolescents try to define who they are by experimenting with their appearance. Remember that rebellious stages will pass.

Discovering sex

During puberty, as their bodies change rapidly, adolescents often vacillate between painful self-consciousness and intense self-absorption. Both boys and girls may preen and strut, giggle and flirt, or become despondent over their appearance.

It can be difficult for you as a parent to cope with the growing sexuality of your adolescent, partly because his or her experimental behavior is a reminder that you, too, were once young and over-whelmed by sexual feelings, and also because you feel you have lost your carefree, innocent child. You may also be genuinely concerned for your child's welfare during this difficult time. What can you do?

• Try to ensure that your son or daughter is emotionally prepared for an adult sexual life.

• Don't think he or she doesn't think about sex. Instead, make sure your son and daughter know about sex, love, and reliable contraception.

• Bear in mind that your own attitudes and emotional history will influence your child.

• Let your son or daughter develop at an independent pace, and respect his or her privacy.

TEENAGERS IN TROUBLE

Your child may struggle through this difficult period. Be aware of the following points:

• Most teenagers get depressed at some stage; they may withdraw from parents and friends, and become moody. They may be in trouble at school or coping with family problems such as divorce. If your child keeps saying that "it's all hopeless," if he or she stays in bed, "gives up," and appears to be sad, you might consult a counselor.

• Peer pressure, and a desire to experiment, may lead to alcohol or drug abuse. Most teenagers never become addicts, but you should be well informed, and discuss the risks with your teenager.

• Eating disorders may sometimes result from a "normal" teenage obsession with dieting and appearance, or from a more deeply rooted problem. Contact your doctor or a counselor.

ADULTHOOD

INEVITABLY, the adolescent becomes an adult, and begins to discover, create, and develop his or her own unique identity. This task is influenced by several factors: environment, the expectations and needs of other people (as well as of the individual), a desire to please others, and, above all, the harsh realities of life in the real world.

Facing reality

As adults, we learn, sometimes painfully, that life isn't easy: We must put up with disappointments, frustrations, and learn through trial and error to avoid mistakes and develop patience—and even then, there are no guarantees that we will get what we want. For some people, having to accept that they're not going to be handed things on a platter, or may have to settle for second-best, is intolerable, and they can spend many years rebelling against the realities of life.

If you can manage to cope with disappointment, you can move forward, developing more skills and confidence, discovering what you are good at and what your weaknesses are. Such lessons are invaluable: Without them, you run the risk of falling back on a child's view of the world, refusing to accept the necessity of adjusting your dreams and aspirations.

Leaving home and finding work

In our late teens or early twenties, most of us step out bravely from the family home—not wanting to show our anxiety and feelings of loss and loneliness—to become responsible adults. One of the main ways we do this is through work and career, and strive to earn enough to support ourselves. Having been dependent on our parents for a long time, this is a tremendous step.

Work can be a valuable way to find out who you are and what you want from life. As well as the means to become financially independent, a job provides much of a young adult's social life. It's a way of experimenting with your talents and social abilities, and is where you meet friends, often forming relationships that last a lifetime.

Relationships and commitment

As adolescents, people tend to idealize another person, or fall in love with only *part* of them, such as their physical attractiveness. As we get older, we learn, mainly through mistakes, what kind of people we're most compatible with, and thus learn to love the whole person—with their good and bad traits. We also learn to show love and respect in order to be treated the same way.

For many people, adulthood ends a long search to find someone to love and share their life with, a search that frequently culminates in marriage. Others, however, may choose to remain single or

LEARNING TO COMPROMISE

Compromise is one of the hardest lessons in life. One of the skills you will need to acquire as an adult is how to harmonize your goals with those of other people, including work colleagues, friends, and marital partners.

This may be very difficult for someone who believes that adults should be allowed to do whatever they want. The thrill of being on your own will be countered by the realization that other freedoms and gratifications will have to be re-evaluated, postponed, or completely given up.

Unless you want to risk loneliness, you will have to learn to listen, share, allow other people to be themselves, and commit yourself to finding solutions to mutual problems.

As well as creating workable solutions that you and other people can happily act on (or can live with), you will also need to learn how to communicate your expectations and intentions clearly and diplomatically. Remember that you have to learn how to *listen* to others and respect their point of view before you can learn how to compromise.

childless. The desire to commit themselves and to contribute to the world in some way, either by establishing a family or through work, is what most adults think is meaningful and important.

More than anything else, being an adult means having the inner strength and confidence to be who you are, taking risks and trusting in your judgment that you know what is best for you. Being an adult also means being resilient, creative, and childlike enough to let yourself be curious and excited by life's possibilities.

To compromise or rebel?
You may have wanted to be a rock star when you were 16, but needed to compromise to earn a living. You can still find ways to be who you "really" are.

MIDLIFE RE-EVALUATION

BY THE TIME you hit your thirties, you'll probably have heard all about the "midlife crisis." You may have some idea of the issues you might have to cope with because you've had to face the fact that, in certain areas of your life, things have not turned out the way you had hoped. For example, you may not have reached the professional level you aspired to, or you may find yourself single beyond the age you planned to marry. There *are* definite phases in our lives, times that involve major changes in our bodies and, more significantly, in our emotional and mental development. Some of these changes are beyond our control.

Growing in strength to cope

As you grow up, physical growth is matched by intellectual and emotional growth. Indeed, the first half of life is spent in *learning* and *acquiring*. From the moment of birth, you acquire skills, ideas, beliefs, relationships, and possibly children. When you reach midlife, however—anytime between the ages of 30 and 60—you reach a threshold, a time when the rate of growth and development changes. Your sense of values may shift as a result. Most importantly, you begin to accept what you may not have accomplished. You learn how to come to terms with your limitations, and with disappointment and loss.

Taking stock

Midlife is when you realize, perhaps for the first time, that you will not live for ever. People who feel they're doing something fulfilling at this stage do not regret that they "don't have enough time" because their days are full and purposeful, but others feel desperate about the lack of joy in their lives, or are overcome with feelings of futility.

A time to reflect and look forward
Like the mythological figure Janus, who could look in two different directions, you can look forward and back in time to re-evaluate your accomplishments and plan future goals.

It might be helpful to recall the Roman god Janus. A two-headed guardian of gateways and crossroads, Janus was the patron god of beginnings and endings who could see forward and back in time. The Romans did not worship youth, but prized instead the accomplishments of maturity. Midlife under the helpful gaze of Janus was seen as an opportunity to acknowledge the passage of time through study,

reflection, and a re-evaluation of what was important, especially the reality of time passing. During a "midlife crisis," desperation and frustration may trigger hasty decisions, such as the abandonment of a job or marriage. If, however, you view midlife as a turning point rather than a crisis, you can ensure that you take the time to consider the changes that will enrich your life in the future.

HOW THE BODY CHANGES

As well as the normal effects of ageing, midlife brings major changes for both men and women as the production of hormones slows down.

The female menopause
The "change of life" for women occurs when levels of estrogen, the female hormone, become lower; menstrual periods stop and a woman is no longer fertile. For some women, this turning point precipitates not only mood swings and night sweats but a deep depression, especially if a woman has always wanted children or has defined herself solely as a mother. Even if there are only mild physical symptoms, menopause is still a significant time of every woman's life.

Hormone replacement therapy (HRT) may greatly contribute to a woman's health and well-being, as can vitamins, herbal supplements, and a positive attitude. HRT must be given under a doctor's care and supervision, since there is a slightly greater risk of some types of cancer.

Men change, too
The "male menopause," sometimes called the "andropause," is less dramatic than the complete cessation of menstrual periods, and occurs later in life: Symptoms, such as lethargy, anxiety, and night sweats, are not usually apparent until a man is in his mid fifties. Hormone levels in men also fluctuate. Levels of testosterone, produced by the testes, slowly diminish, while another hormone, sex hormone binding globulin (SHBG), increases and absorbs testosterone so that less of this substance circulates in the body.

The most troublesome symptom, loss of libido and potency, affects about 20 percent of men in their sixties. It can be treated with synthetic testosterone, either in pill form or as an implant placed under the skin. One side-effect is a rise of fat levels in the blood, which increases the risk of blood clots forming or of a heart attack.

As with the menopause, vitamins and herbal supplements can help to restore energy.

MIDLIFE REJUVENATION

Although midlife is, without doubt, a time to recognize the inevitability of ageing, and to re-evaluate key areas of your life experience, it need not be a time solely of loss. In fact, for many people, it offers an opportunity to reclaim parts of themselves that might have been buried under the responsibilities of work and family. The urgency of rediscovery is sometimes fueled by the awareness of death and loss: Parents and friends become ill or die, and you may also be aware that you are definitely slowing down, certainly no longer invincible or in complete control. What can mitigate the growing awareness of loss?

From remorse to pleasure

In his book *The Course of Life*, psychoanalyst George Pollock has suggested that midlife is marked by what he calls the "mourning-liberation process," which begins with the insight that certain things—who we wanted to be, what we had hoped to gain (professional recognition, a large and stable family)—are no longer possible. The strength needed to cope with such losses of possibility may be immense, but when reality is faced and accepted, and when unattainable hopes are mourned, it is possible to move beyond sadness toward new horizons and aspirations. A new relationship with the past is constructed: When the past can be accepted as concluded, the future opens up.

Pollock suggests that such honesty generates new interests and activities, and that "serenity, joy, pleasure, and excitement come into being." Instead of being withdrawn and depressed, or choosing to remain isolated, older people may feel rejuvenated, full of "humor, wisdom, and the capacity to contemplate their own impermanence."

Time flies...
Because time becomes very precious in midlife, focus on the people, activities, and values that are most important to you.

Enjoying work

Many people in their forties and fifties have to cope with the realization that they have come as far as possible in their careers. For some, this can be a time of recognition and the consolidation of authority. For others, this transitional time is rocky. They may compete with younger people, feel frustrated, or be laid off. Even in these difficult situations,

RESPECT YOUR INNER LIFE

At midlife, many people feel a greater need to fulfill themselves, and discover that their inner life, their dreams, and their imagination become more wide-ranging and vivid. It's never too late to give more time to expressing yourself; many artists, such as Leonardo da Vinci, who continued to produce brilliant work well into his sixties, have been at their most creative in their later years. How can you enrich your own life and enhance your creativity?
• Try to discover what your real needs and desires are, and what you can realistically accomplish.
• Don't be afraid to try something you've always wanted to do.
• Don't dismiss your intuitive hunches or daydreams.
• Keep a diary of your dreams, especially during periods of confusion when they can provide clues about what you might do.

however, there can be an opportunity to change direction, or perhaps to get a "second wind." This is particularly true now that society is changing: Very few people work at one job or for one company for their entire lives, and the population of most Western societies, although ageing, is also better educated and in better health. Technological changes may be learned more quickly by younger people, but studies show that any deficit of learning speed in older people is compensated for by their experience, creativity, and sense of responsibility.

Relationships and the midlife crisis

The prevailing myth of the midlife crisis is that a seemingly well-adjusted man runs off with a much younger woman, or an older divorcee desperately seeks to remarry. The marital breakdown that seems an inevitable part of this myth is compounded by another fallacy: that adults past the biological age of reproduction have no sex life. Most research into sexual behavior focuses on young adults, not necessarily adults over the age of 40.

• Are you happy with the proportion of time you spend with friends and on your own? You may need greater solitude in order to pursue creative hobbies.
• Remember that creativity does not mean that you have to produce a work of art. You can create a wide circle of friends and family, enjoy volunteer work, or undertake a long course of study. In fact, anything that contributes to your vitality, sense of purpose, and joy is creative.

Enhanced creativity
In midlife, you may feel a greater need for inner reflection, and to explore your creativity and find ways of expressing yourself.

There can be little doubt that the boundaries of relationships shift when children leave home. A husband and wife may have become very different people, which may generate vehement arguments —and they may find that they have little in common any more, or ask, "What can I look forward to?"

New scenarios

One of the benefits of a long relationship, especially after children leave home, is that partners have more time to be attentive and responsive to each other's needs, some of which have probably changed over the years.

Studies of midlife suggest that this period marks the need for the *new*. Although new expectations and needs may follow in the wake of midlife re-evaluation, these do not necessarily mean new partners. Some researchers have proposed that emotional changes reflect the fact that, once children have left home, there may be a shift in gender identities: Men may want to redefine their paternal roles and explore their more passive, intuitive sides, while women seek to become *less* passive, less concerned with domesticity, and more active in the world. These changes affect everything from domestic arrangements to the expression of sexual and emotional needs.

There is a risk of marital breakdown (see "Divorce," pp. 38–39), but it is not an inevitable consequence of midlife. If you and your partner are flexible, basically companionable, and trusting, you'll probably find it easier to allow each other freedom to explore and express facets of your temperament that need to grow. During this rediscovery, there may be many new opportunities to create intimacy and to share interesting pursuits. There is also great satisfaction in having one partner with whom you have a long, shared history.

THE LATER YEARS

IN SOME NOMADIC or farming communities, ancestors are sometimes deified and regarded as powerful protectors. Elderly people are respected and sometimes revered, and age is equated with the wisdom of life experience and self-acceptance. Is this wisdom really attainable?

Changing relationships

The great fear of the later years is decreasing mobility and isolation, especially if families and close friends live far away. Loss of health, or of close relatives to take on the role of carer, may necessitate moving to a retirement community, sheltered accommodation, or a nursing home.

Even when this occurs, it is still possible to build relationships. These communities, for example, or friends of similar age, offer many people the chance to create very strong friendships based on common interests and affection.

Accepting loss and mortality

The depression older people may experience is not only due to physical decline, such as having to cope with difficulty walking or illness. Because they have fewer responsibilities to distract them from their inner life, there are many previous losses they were unable to think about or mourn at the time they occurred, but that now need to be dealt with. Indeed, many activities of adulthood can be used as defenses against acknowledging deeper feelings and needs; in the absence of outer concerns, older people have the chance to review their lives.

"SLOW DOWN" DOESN'T MEAN "STOP!"

As with other developmental turning points, there are physical changes to be acknowledged in later years. You may walk more slowly, breathe a little harder, your heart rhythm may change, and your vision and hearing may be less acute. Some people are resigned to these changes and accept them with relative good grace—indeed, some feel relieved that they can "put down their paddle and float," and no longer have to look "perfect" all the time. Others are resentful and fearful of their declining health and independence. What is the best way to cope with your changing body, stamina, and capabilities?

• Accept that you cannot stop the process of ageing. You may be able to delay its effects in some ways, but there is no elixir of eternal youth.
• If any health problems develop, don't pretend that they don't exist. See a doctor and follow his or her recommendations.

• Remain as physically active as possible. Regular moderate exercise, especially walking, is of great benefit. If you are not in the habit of walking, you could team up with a more energetic friend who will encourage you. If you prefer more social activities, you can join a dance or sports group, or an exercise class.
• Decide to take responsibility for your health, fitness, and well-being—including your diet and mental outlook—and make the most of your life. Health is often a reflection of a positive frame of mind.

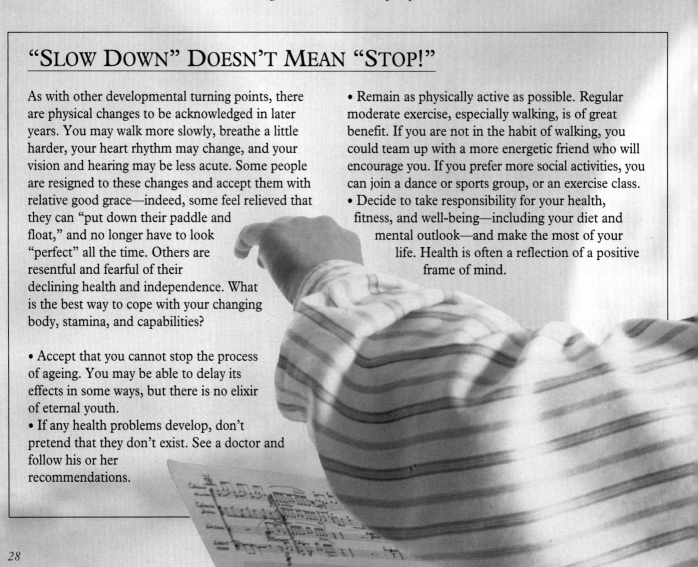

Although there are some older people who resign themselves to a bleak future and become rigid or embittered in their outlook, there are many others who look forward to having the time and space to explore and learn—and they thrive. There *is* a wisdom that comes with age, and it often depends on self-acceptance and a detachment from what was previously considered important, such as work or social status. For many people, warmth, tenderness, and intimacy become important to establish or sustain. Self-forgiveness and freeing yourself from regrets about what you can no longer remedy are important steps toward inner freedom and the feeling that life is worthwhile. Some people have a profound religious or philosophical belief that helps sustain them, but even without such beliefs, it's possible for most people to reach a state of greater calm and understanding, and a feeling of deep gratitude for the lives they have had.

Conducting yourself
As an older person, you will have gained an awareness of the rhythms of life, and have much to offer the wider community. It takes strength to retain an independent and questing spirit, but you will benefit from maintaining an optimistic outlook.

CHAPTER TWO

CHANGE AND PERSONAL CRISIS

SOME CRISES DEEPLY AFFECT our sense of security and identity, undermining the assumptions we have about ourselves and the world around us. This chapter looks at some of the most serious crises, those that may leave us, or those we love, feeling fragile, confused, deeply disappointed or sad, and frequently quite lonely. It also explores ways of working through them, of coping with their after-effects, and of gaining strength from your experience.

Can you recognize the warning signs of a potential breakdown in a significant relationship? In the article "Check Your Relationship," pages 32-33, a questionnaire will help you to identify areas of possible incompatibility or conflict between you and your partner, such as money, sex, and frustrating patterns of communication. You may then find a way of tackling problems openly and honestly with your partner, possibly defusing a crisis before it unexpectedly explodes. If your relationship ends, however, you may have a rare opportunity to reflect on your life and what you want. You may have the chance to develop your own inner resources, value your own company, and pursue what may be long-abandoned dreams and ambitions (see "Single Again," pp. 40-41).

Losing your job can precipitate a crisis, making you feel like a failure, but it can also stimulate you to grow in new directions. "Dealing with Unemployment," pages 42-43, offers practical guidance on creating new opportunities for yourself. Unemployment may also generate financial havoc, so "Getting Out of Debt," pages 44-45, explains simple strategies for managing your money.

If someone you love dies, you may feel anger and guilt, as well as sadness and grief (see "Death and Mourning," pp. 50-51). These feelings can be distressing, but with time and understanding, you can regain strength and rebuild your life. You will also learn to appreciate the precious but limited time you have with friends and companions who care for you.

Being the victim of a personal assault, or being involved in an accident, can make you feel that the world is a dangerous place. "Coping with Crime," pages 54-55, offers advice to help you recover and to protect yourself. In more extreme cases, particularly after serious accidents or large-scale disasters, people may suffer from post-traumatic stress (pp. 60-61). Help from counselors, or from support groups of fellow sufferers, often puts people back on the road to recovery.

EVERY LIFE IS TOUCHED BY A CRISIS AT SOME POINT,

BUT THERE ARE MANY PRACTICAL AND EMOTIONAL STRATEGIES

THAT CAN HELP GET YOU THROUGH.

CHECK YOUR RELATIONSHIP

Even the happiest, most rewarding relationships are not without their troubles. Working through difficulties can help to forge a stronger bond between partners. If problems are left unaddressed, however, they can lead to a buildup of frustration, anger, or resentment, which can seriously undermine trust and affection. The questionnaire below will help you to assess your relationship and to recognize areas of potential conflict so that you can more easily resolve any tensions. Answer the questions as honestly as you can, then turn to page 140 for comments.

Communication

1. Do you feel that you and your partner spend as much time talking as you'd like? When you talk, do you feel rushed?

2. Are you honest with your partner? Do you explain how you think and feel?

3. Do you listen attentively when your partner says how he/she thinks and feels?

4. Do you accept your partner's opinions and feelings even when different from your own?

5. Do you try to sort out your differences by talking honestly together?

6. Do you nag in order to wear your partner down and get what you want?

7. Does your partner nag you in order to get what he/she wants?

8. Do you change the subject if he/she raises an issue you don't want to confront?

9. Do you give your partner the "silent treatment" when you are angry?

10. Does your partner give you the "silent treatment" when he/she is angry?

11. Are you verbally abusive when angry?

12. Is your partner verbally abusive or threatening when he/she is angry?

13. Do you agree on important issues, such as raising children and basic values?

14. Do you trust your partner with your innermost feelings?

15. Do you and your partner often make each other laugh?

Money

1. Do you feel happy about the level of contribution that your partner makes to the household expenses?

2. Do you and your partner agree on how money should be spent?

3. Do you use money or presents as bribes to get what you want?

4. Does your partner use money or presents as bribes to get what he/she wants?

5. Do you trust your partner with money?

6. Do you resent the fact that your partner doesn't earn more money?

7. Does your partner resent the fact that you don't earn more money?

8. Do you sometimes spontaneously buy your partner surprise gifts?

9. Does your partner sometimes buy you surprise gifts, and do you enjoy them?

10. Do you think your partner is selfish with money? If so, why is he/she like that?

11. Do you argue over financial matters?

12. Do you sometimes lie to your partner about money or expenditures?

13. Do you ever suspect your partner of lying to you about money?

14. Do you resent what your partner spends his/her money on?

15. Do you think that financial considerations are an important aspect of why you continue to stay together, even if you're not entirely happy?

Sex

1. Are you satisfied with the frequency of your lovemaking?

2. Can you express your sexual needs to your partner or do you feel that he/she should know how to please you without your saying?

3. Do you still find your partner attractive and sexually desirable?

4. Do you feel under pressure to engage in sex acts you don't enjoy?

5. Are you a generous lover? Are you prepared to do things that don't necessarily excite you but please your partner?

6. Does your partner know how and where you like to be touched?

7. Do you punish your partner by withholding sex when you are angry? Could you express your feelings more directly?

8. Does your partner withhold sex to punish you when he/she is angry?

9. Do you use sex as a bribe to get what you want when you know your partner would not agree?

10. Do you and your partner ever set time aside for lovemaking?

11. Do you feel closer and more loving toward your partner after sex?

12. Is sex the only way you show your partner physical affection? Do you feel awkward expressing affection in other ways?

13. Is sex the only way your partner shows you physical affection? Would you like to be kissed and cuddled more without feeling it would always lead to sex?

14. Do you have to fantasize about something or someone else to get aroused?

15. Do you both enjoy maintaining close contact after sex, or do you move apart almost immediately and feel isolated?

Personal satisfaction

1. Do you genuinely value your partner as a person and as a close friend?

2. Do you feel your partner values you as a person and as a close friend?

3. Do you feel that you respect your partner's opinions and values?

4. Do you feel your opinions and values are listened to and respected?

5. Do you feel that you tend to take your partner for granted?

6. Do you feel that your partner tends to take you for granted?

7. Do you feel that the burden of household chores falls mainly on you? If so, do you resent it, and would you like this to change?

8. Do you feel that your needs and aspirations typically take second place to your partner's? Has it always been like this?

9. Do you feel insecure about your partner's love and constantly need reassurance?

10. Do you suffer from excessive jealousy?

11. Does your partner make you feel inferior?

12. Do you feel your partner brings out the best in you? Does he/she actively encourage you?

13. Does your partner satisfy most of your emotional needs?

14. Do you feel your partner is an ally and that you could rely on him/her for total support?

15. Do you feel your relationship enriches your life, or is it holding you back?

Facing the truth
Making an honest appraisal of your relationship can help you to identify and work on areas of conflict, thereby averting a potential crisis.

RELATIONSHIPS IN CRISIS

M OST OF US enter a relationship with high hopes of long-lasting happiness. Few people sincerely commit themselves to another person while also anticipating the day it will end. If our first serious relationship fails, we learn only too painfully that our hopes may not be realized. Relationships *do* end, some at the first sign of serious trouble, others only after years of what may have been in many ways a close and happy union When a relationship breaks down, emotions are plunged into turmoil. People feel deep unhappiness, as well as the anger, jealousy, self-doubt, and grief that accompany any major loss. This can be true even if the relationship has been a relatively short one.

A damaging ideal?

The myth of the perfect relationship is a popular one. How tempting it can be to believe that, if we find the "right" partner, our problems will be solved and our lives sorted out. Even if you consciously regard this expectation as unrealistic, you may still feel deeply disappointed when problems arise. But no long-term relationship can avoid problems altogether, nor should it; while love remains untried and overprotected from reality, it will always be fragile. A strong and rewarding relationship depends on our ability to be flexible and understanding, to negotiate difficulties, and to adjust to changes.

Why relationships change

There are many reasons why relationships break down. In some cases, problems may fester for years, so that anger, frustration, and resentment build up. In others, a sudden change such as the revelation of an affair, or a gambling or alchohol problem, destroys trust and plunges the relationship into crisis. Another reason might simply be long-standing boredom, or the fact that partners change in different ways over time and are no longer compatible. Whatever the cause, however, the consequences are the same—talking is replaced by silence or arguments, closeness is replaced by estrangement, and companionship and respect are slowly eroded.

Crumbling foundations?
Problems in a relationship should be acknowledged and resolved; otherwise, the bond between two people may crumble and collapse.

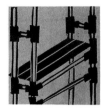

Preventive measures

If relations between you and your partner have become strained, try to air your feelings before they become explosive or deep-rooted. Arrange an unhurried time to talk, and encourage your partner to share how he or she feels. Without talking, you cannot know what the other person thinks, feels, hopes, fears, or expects. Good communication is not always easy, however; you both need to learn how to express yourselves as clearly as possible, and to listen carefully to each other. Try to avoid making assumptions about how the other person thinks and feels, and accept that there may be more than one "truth."

Family and friends

Love relationships are not the only ones that suffer from problems; difficulties with relatives or friends can also be very serious, and may lead to long-term estrangements or bitter disputes. These may stem from many causes, such as resentment over one person's success or good fortune, a conflict of loyalties, a betrayal of trust, or even a misunderstanding.

As in partnerships, the best way to rebuild bridges is through a genuine attempt at communication, although you may have to regain harmony step by step. It may be easier to take the first step with a letter; then you can consider exactly what you want to say and how best to say it without being hastily challenged or interrupted.

Recognizing the end

Not all relationships can be mended and saved; in some cases, the conflict is so damaging—if there has been mental or physical abuse, for example—that reconciliation may be out of the question. Or you may simply have developed in such different ways that you no longer have much in common. There are also relationships that, although they are enjoyable in some ways, actually exert a negative effect on us and our lives, perhaps damaging our self-esteem or restricting our development. In these cases, once you have learned to let them go, you can move forward.

INFIDELITY

Sexual infidelity is potentially the most difficult crisis that any relationship may have to face. To discover that your partner has slept with someone else is the most painful betrayal. It is particularly devastating if the infidelity is a long-standing affair, but a one-night stand can also damage trust. Most of us meet other people we find attractive, but while we are committed to our relationship we probably refrain from trying to take matters any further. When we do give in to temptation, it usually indicates that there are problems in our principal relationship that need to be addressed.

Causes of infidelity

In *The Relate Guide to Better Relationships*, author Sarah Litvinoff explains some of the main reasons why people are unfaithful to their partners:

Protest: If you are going through an acrimonious time, rowing about money, the division of chores, or other domestic issues, you or your partner might feel entitled to look for and receive understanding, appreciation, and respite elsewhere.

Insecurity: Insecurity can drive you or your partner to seek reassurance outside the relationship. This could happen if a man feels pushed aside by the birth of a baby, for example, or if one person feels he or she takes second place to his or her partner's work. Feeling vulnerable about ageing and loss of sexual attractiveness can also tempt people to seek excitement and attention in an affair.

Sex: If your sex life has become dull, unsatisfying, predictable, or simply non-existent, the idea of an affair can seem an exciting and irresistible temptation that will restore your vitality.

Growing apart: An affair can seem to offer understanding and communication if you and your partner have grown in different directions or feel disconnected from each other and no longer talk openly together.

Relationship breakdown: This occurs when one or both of you feel that the relationship is over. An affair at this stage is often used as a way out or as a means of precipitating a separation.

Multiple loves
Having an affair undermines a person's principal relationship and allows him or her to avoid closeness and commitment.

Are you prone to temptation?

In addition, some people are "affair-prone" even if they really have no intention of splitting up from their partner. There are two main reasons for this:

Excitement: For some people, the intense excitement of a new sexual encounter is like a drug. The "excitement junkie" might have a series of clandestine affairs or one-night stands, or both.

Fear of intimacy: Some people find the intimacy of a serious relationship too uncomfortable to handle; they fear they will be engulfed by the other person, or that if they let a partner get close and know what they are really like, then the partner will reject or abandon them. If they are conducting a long-term affair, they have, in effect, two part-time relationships. This provides them with the measure of distance they feel they need, and a feeling of being in control of the situation—or the other people.

A case of revenge

When Naomi and Vincent's marriage began showing cracks, Vincent took a job with long hours, and, to avoid facing their problems, was often away. Naomi's resentment at his withdrawal vented itself in bitter reproaches, and their sex life ground to a halt. She started an affair in order to get back at Vincent. She told Vincent about it during an argument and, after the initial shock, he felt both miserable and angry. He realized that he didn't want his marriage to end, however, and agreed to have counseling with Naomi. He came to accept that his inability to talk about his feelings had frozen Naomi out. For her part, Naomi could see that her verbal assaults had only driven him further away.

With the help of the counselor, they learned to communicate effectively and agreed on ways they could rebuild their trust and help meet each other's needs.

MAKING A FRESH START

In some cases, the damage done by an affair may be too deep to be overcome, and both partners will have a better chance of happiness apart. If you don't want to part, however, and are willing to work to stay together, it is possible to create a new, stronger relationship—but bear in mind that it is a lot more difficult to restore trust once it has been broken than it is to establish in the first place. Both of you will need many of the qualities listed below to help build this new relationship and to see you both through the difficult and confusing times:

• **Openness:** Expressing thoughts and feelings helps your partner understand your needs.

• **Flexibility:** Be prepared to be adaptable, and to work at finding ways to create a different kind of relationship—one that suits you both.

• **Sensitivity:** You need to be sensitive to and tolerant of your partner's needs and feelings of anger, resentment, or rejection.

• **Respect:** Give your partner respect, just as you would like it yourself. Show how much you value him or her and how highly you rate your partner as an important part of your life.

• **Commitment:** Remember that a half-hearted attempt to patch things up is doomed to failure.

• **Patience:** Don't be too hard on yourselves. You can't rebuild a relationship overnight. If you have setbacks, don't give up hope.

DIVORCE

Divorce is devastating. No matter how bad the relationship, or who instigated the separation, the emotional and practical impact on your life is enormous. Losing your partner can lead to other losses: your identity as one of a couple, perhaps, or contact with your partner's family or with your mutual friends; your new single status may threaten other couples who may withdraw from you a little. Finally, and most painfully, divorce may deprive you of daily contact with your children.

Shock waves

The end of a major relationship is like a bereavement. You feel numb and dazed—especially if you have been left—as well as angry, sad, and depressed. You may fluctuate between confident days when you feel you can build a good future, and sad days when memories plunge you into despair. Such ups and downs are normal but should gradually lessen. If your depression does not lift with time, and you continue to be obsessed with the relationship, fantasizing about revenge, or reconciliation, you are stopping yourself from creating a new and richer life for the future.

Stuck in the past

"An ongoing connection with your ex-spouse or former life that keeps you agitated or depressed, unhappy and stuck in the past" is how author Anne N. Walther describes the syndrome of "divorce hangover." She cites the case of Bonnie, who has not seen her ex-husband since they divorced six years ago, but thinks about him constantly. She asks mutual friends about whom he is dating, his work situation, and other details. When she is not consumed with anger, Bonnie weeps inconsolably.

Divorce hangover is particularly acute when people continue to have sex with ex-partners; they are refusing to accept that the relationship is over. Claire, for example, often had sex with her ex-husband when he visited their children. Her depression lifted only when counseling helped her to analyze the relationship and understand the reasons for the end of her marriage. She realized that while she continued to have sex with her ex-spouse, she would never be emotionally or mentally free to start a new life or relationship. If you have a divorce hangover, you can cure it, although you will need patience, perseverance, and a real desire to recover. Anne Walther's ten-step plan (see right) can help you start on the road to a new life.

Prepare to rebuild
When a relationship ends, it may feel as if your whole life is in ruins, but with strength and a positive attitude you can build yourself a new life.

CURING THE HANGOVER

You do not have to let regrets or bitterness about the end of a marriage or long-term relationship overshadow your life; you can learn from your experience, cherish the good times that you did have, and focus your energies on your future.

Step 1: Take control of your emotional turmoil. You need to move from *feelings* to *rational thinking*. When an emotion boils over, try to identify it. What are you feeling? Give yourself time and space to think it through. Understanding your feelings will help you feel you're regaining control of your life.

Step 2: Gain a deeper understanding of the relationship. What attracted you to each other? What worked? What went wrong? Could you have behaved differently, or could there have been a different outcome? Uncovering the truth and facing it squarely will help you avoid the same pitfalls in a future relationship.

Step 3: Take stock of your losses. These may be both emotional and practical. By deciding to accept them, and allowing yourself time to grieve, you hasten your recovery from disappointment.

Step 4: Recognize how self-destructive anger is. Such feelings only prolong your hangover. You have to make a conscious decision to redirect negative feelings when they resurface.

Step 5: Unmask your hangover. You may be hiding unresolved pain, which surfaces as anger. If, for example, you still blame your ex's new partner for the breakup, you will be unable to examine and understand your own role in the relationship, and so won't be able to move on emotionally.

Step 6: Let go of feelings of guilt, failure, or blame. No matter how badly you have been treated, now is the time to step out of the role of victim, and take charge of your life, while letting your ex-partner take responsibility for his or her own life, too.

Step 7: Accept that your former life and identity in the partnership no longer exist. Realize that there is more to you than your marriage. Letting go often hurts, but you will gain a sense of relief and be free to begin anew.

Step 8: Think about the divorce hangover as a process of recovery. During any recovery, there are decisions to be made. One of yours might be, "I'm not meeting enough people, so I'll join a choir/social club/evening class."

Step 9: Turn negative thoughts into positive ones. Positive attitudes create positive behavior. You can change your life by changing the way you think.

Step 10: Rebuild your self-esteem. Divorce can knock your self-esteem, but you can rebuild it. Think about how you are and how you want to be. You can change if you want, but don't expect to be perfect. Don't be afraid to ask for help— from your friends, family, or a counselor.

SINGLE AGAIN

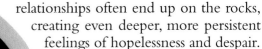

The ending of a relationship, a separation or divorce, or the death of a partner, can unexpectedly return you to a single life. Although this can undoubtedly be traumatic or sad, the belief that your ultimate happiness depends on having that one special person in your life leaves you at the mercy of events that are often beyond your control. The only guarantee of lasting happiness is to develop your inner resources, and being on your own is the ideal opportunity to expand your horizons and discover who you really are and what you want from life.

With a positive attitude, you will gain long-lasting assets: strength, resilience, and wisdom.

First steps

Being single again, even if you have decided this is what you want, can, at first, be bewildering. You may still be feeling the depth of your loss, as well as adjusting to new living patterns. You may have had to take on new practical responsibilities, and miss having someone around to talk to.

To fill your inner emptiness, you may be tempted to throw yourself straight into a new relationship, but expectations of long-lasting happiness, coupled with any emotional defensiveness and confusion about what you want from a relationship, can put a great deal of pressure on your new partner. Hastily begun "transitional" relationships often end up on the rocks, creating even deeper, more persistent feelings of hopelessness and despair.

There is no such thing as instant healing; it takes time, but you can initiate the process by learning to understand your own feelings. This may seem obvious, but perhaps you have never thought deeply about what makes you happy, sad, or angry, or what your emotional needs and expectations of a relationship really are.

Give yourself a treat

Being single again is a chance to learn how to be good to yourself, instead of relying on others. Try to do something nice for yourself each day. See a friend, cook yourself a special meal, or take time for a walk. Try not to indulge in pleasures with negative consequences, such as eating or drinking too much, which might make you feel ill as well as angry and self-critical at your lack of self-control.

Treating yourself is a way of affirming your self-worth, and is a step toward creating your own contentment. Raising your spirits in these small ways prepares you for bigger things.

Alone but not lonely

Everyone feels lonely sometimes, especially if separated from friends and family, but the people who suffer most intensely tend to be those who are less in touch with themselves or more fearful of their independence. This type of loneliness occurs when people feel misunderstood, or are emotionally isolated. It is also felt by people who choose to stay in

Opening doors
Becoming single again can yield many opportunities for you to try new things, such as traveling by yourself and taking up new interests.

unhappy or unrewarding relationships because of their fear of loneliness, believing that even the worst relationship is better than none. This is, however, a self-defeating and unproductive attitude.

Becoming friends with yourself, and learning to enjoy and value your own company are the most fundamental ways to combat loneliness. Whether you are single or not, you should feel happy to pursue your interests or new hobbies on your own.

Your friends can be a source of joy and support, so this is a good time to strengthen your friendships. Learning how to accept their generous offers of help can be an important step toward self-acceptance.

Positively single

According to psychologist Edward E. Jones, our expectations not only affect how we view reality but also affect reality itself; that is, they determine how we behave, and it is our behavior that influences or alters our social environment.

To be positively single, you must expect independence to offer fresh opportunities. For example, to be without a partner means you are free to look at what you want from life and how you want to achieve your goals. Instead of dreading the time you spend alone, see yourself as having the luxury of creative solitude in order to rebuild your life.

Visions and goals generate excitement and purpose, motivating you to try new things. Taking steps in unexpected directions increases your self-esteem, confidence, and sense of your own power.

Going out is good for you

If you wait for a social life to come to you, you may spend a lot of evenings in. Go out and make it happen. Believe that you can create a whole new circle of friends—that there are people out there who want to know you—and it will happen.

Renew contacts with single friends, rediscover your interests, and take up new hobbies, no matter how exotic they seem. Don't be afraid to attend clubs that organize social events for meeting new people. Ultimately, the more positively single you are, the more you will enjoy life and the more likely you are to find yourself in a rewarding relationship with a new and interesting partner.

DEALING WITH UNEMPLOYMENT

A JOB FOR LIFE, in today's changing economic climate, is no longer a realistic expectation. Whereas your grandparents may have worked for one employer for their whole lives, and your parents may have had a few changes of employer within one industry, you may experience not just changes in employer, but changes in career during your working life. Sometimes, these changes may be distressing, the result of unwanted or unforeseen unemployment. However apparent the warning signs may have been, unemployment usually evokes shock, anger, and overwhelming feelings of humiliation and rejection.

But, as in many crises, the threats to your wellbeing can be positive forces for change. If, for example, you have some redundancy money, you can use the time and space to reassess your life, and look for new opportunities. First, however, you have to come to terms with the event, and to understand the emotions and threats you feel.

You may feel like a failure at your job, and therefore that no-one else will want to employ you. You will probably experience anger and outrage, and feel, "It's not fair, why me?" Fear of financial hardship, the loss of respect of friends, family, and colleagues, and the loss of status can all add to your distress. You may fear that you will be unable to provide for your family. Some or all of these factors will undermine your self-esteem, but will be harder to bear if you have had few interests outside of work, and your work was the focus of your life and source of your sense of purpose and self-worth.

Some of these emotions may be bound up with the fact that society generally places more importance on what you do than on who you are. Don't forget that you are fundamentally still the person you were, with all the qualities, skills, and talents you had before. What has happened has not changed who you are, only what you do. This event may be the opportunity to take the plunge, change direction, and have the life you always really wanted.

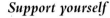

Support yourself
If you are out of work, being flexible and willing to try new things and learn new skills will help ensure that you are your own best support.

Moving on

If you lose your job, you need to be honest with yourself and others. Denial will only take away your power to act positively. Tell your partner, family, and friends right away, and ask for their support. Telling others also helps the reality of your situation to sink in and the shock will start to fade. You will then be more able to evaluate your skills and clarify your future goals, which will enable you to move on.

The loss of a daily structure can be very unsettling, so try to devise a regular timetable. Remaining in the habit of getting up at a regular time, and not going to bed too late, will make it easier to adjust when you are back in work, and helps maintain your morale. Divide the day into sections and plan your activities, which may include action on the job front, relaxation and exercise, time with family and friends, training or education, and jobs around the home and garden that you never had time for. Re-evaluate your job history and qualifications; changing technology has altered many types of job. Consider your age, temperament, and aptitude, and see if you can discover a "market niche" into which you could comfortably fit.

Keep believing in yourself

Fight negative feelings by doing things you enjoy, especially those you had little time for while working. Taking on a challenge—learning something new, especially a job-related skill, or devising a new health and fitness regimen—will give you a feeling of achievement, and help to rebuild your confidence. This is an essential strategy for recovering self-esteem, and will help you to feel positive and optimistic about going for interviews.

Looking good makes you feel good, so don't neglect your appearance, and keep dressing as if for work: You never know whom you might bump into, and it's important to appear competent and professional. Everyone you meet is a contact, and networking can bring new opportunities. Consider possible new careers, read about them, and talk to others in similar jobs. Talk positively about your situation by saying things like, "I'm working on what I want to do next," or "I'm planning a change of career." Finally, remember to thank people for any advice and efforts they make on your behalf.

WHAT STEPS TO TAKE

Planning and taking specific practical action will help you feel that you are still in charge of your life, rather than at its mercy, and can improve your situation, too.

• Talk over the practical and emotional implications of your new situation with your partner or family—it affects them, too.
• Discuss what you might want to do in future and how this will fit in with those around you.
• Contact the government unemployment agency for information about training. Charitable advisory services may also have helpful ideas.
• Contact your tax office. You may be entitled to rebates. Get any financial help you can.
• Look at your finances and draw up a budget plan so you know exactly where you are. Talk to your bank manager before problems arise.
• Rewrite your resumé or c.v. Make a list of your strengths and abilities.
• Ask for advice from friends and family. They may help you identify qualities and skills you may not recognize. Have a brainstorming session with a friend to come up with ideas of new avenues to try.
• Take adult education classes—to gain new skills, to improve your job prospects, or to find a new sense of enjoyment and purpose.

GETTING OUT OF DEBT

I F YOU WORRY about getting overdrawn now and again, or sometimes run up too much on your credit card, or are extravagant once in a while, you're like many other people and will probably never get into serious debt. Constant overspending, however, will inevitably cause debt to creep up unexpectedly, causing you shame and distress. Such behavior may also seriously undermine the well-being and security of your family.

Do you know how to budget?

Have you ever worked out what you need to earn to pay for the necessities of life, let alone the luxuries? If not, now is the time. Use the budget plan on the next page to get a clear picture of how your earnings match up with what you spend.

• First, start by listing all your regular bills, such as rent/mortgage, insurance, and utilities. You can use last year's bills to work out an average monthly expenditure, allowing for any increase in consumption or price.

• Next, subtract your monthly outgoings from your income. What is left is your disposable income, and should pay for clothes, going out, holidays, and all those little extras, which can often add up to more than you might imagine. Keeping receipts for every cash purchase for a week will help you identify areas where money tends to slip through your fingers.

• If what you spend exceeds your estimates, you should consider cutting back in certain areas.

Face facts

If you are in debt, or your budget plan shows that you could be heading that way, stop and take stock right away. Delay and denial will only make matters worse. Be honest with your family and friends, especially those who may be affected.

Using the budget plan, see whether you have any spare income, which could go toward paying off debts, or consider where you could make economies. Be sure to discuss each item with anyone else who will be affected, and consider the implications carefully.

A steady climb
Once you devise a realistic budget, you can work toward minimizing your debts.

Selling the car may produce cash and reduce outlay, but combined family travel may actually cost more. Instead of losing the benefits of the telephone, agree to make only essential outgoing calls.

The aim is to reduce your expenditure so that it is less than your income, using any surplus to pay off your debts or to save. A contingency fund for emergencies, such as medical care, unexpected repairs to your home, or special occasions can often save the day.

The best advice

If such cost-cutting is unlikely to resolve your economic situation in a few months, consider taking these additional steps:

• Talk to your bank manager and find out how he or she can help. A temporary overdraft or a loan at a lower interest rate may be the best way to deal with any credit card debts, which often have very high interest rates.

• Talk to your mortgage company. They may be willing to accept reduced or interest-only payments for a short period.

• Talk to the utility companies. If you are honest about your situation, you may find they are willing to allow you to pay off your debts gradually. Provided you contact them, they are unlikely to cut you off.

• If you owe any taxes, contact the government collection agencies, who may be less flexible than banks or utility companies. You should put any debts in this group at the top of your payment priorities.

• You may also find it helpful to consult a debt-counseling service, and get advice on any legal implications of your debts.

• Always remember the three vital elements to maintaining a debt-free life: Keep in touch with your money, always face the facts, and take any action required immediately. Then a crisis is unlikely to escalate into a catastrophe.

YOUR BUDGET PLAN

Use the plan below and fill in amounts for your monthly income and expenditure.

Expenditure

Essential		*Optional*	
Rent/mortgage	....	Contingency	....
Local taxes	....	Clothes	....
Heating/lighting	....	Holidays	....
Water	....	Outings	....
Telephone	....		
TV	....	SUB-TOTAL	....
Insurance	....		
Car (fuel, repairs, etc.)	....	**Income**	....
Travel (whole family)	....	Balance	
Food	....	(credit/debit)	....
Other			
(standing orders, etc.)	....	**Debts**	
		Bank	....
SUB-TOTAL	......	Credit cards	....
		Other	....

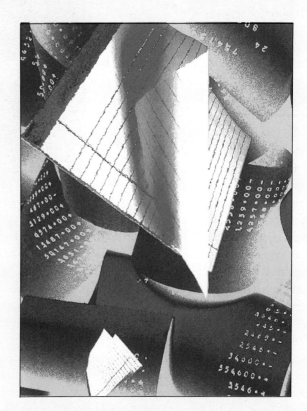

COPING WITH ILLNESS

SERIOUS ILLNESS OR INJURY—either your own or that of a loved one—can plunge you both into a crisis. As each person struggles with the practical and emotional consequences, a relationship can be thrown off balance and the hidden dynamics revealed for the first time. Over-dependent partners may panic at the sudden need to make decisions alone, and long-standing communication problems may need to be addressed.

For example, Jenny was the family linchpin who saw to it that everything at home ran smoothly. But after a hysterectomy at 37, she fell into a deep depression, and couldn't get out of bed. Her husband, David, took time off work to look after her and their three children, aged nine, seven, and four. As well as worrying about Jenny—especially her emotional state—he, for the first time, had to contend with the full burden of chores and child care. The two older children, upset about their mother, became quarrelsome and uncooperative. The youngest child expressed his distress with frequent tantrums and bed-wetting.

David couldn't really understand Jenny's depression, and thought she could take a more positive attitude—no more need for contraception, for example. He found it hard to talk with the children, and realized that Jenny was the one they usually turned to. Her illness had highlighted the shortcomings of his own relationship with his children. Although stressed by the extra work, he resolved to improve this relationship, and worked hard at building greater trust and understanding with them. Jenny's doctor suggested she see a counselor; she found it helpful to discuss her worries and fears with someone experienced in dealing with such problems. She was soon up and about again, but David continued to be more involved with the house and children, and Jenny had more time for other interests outside being a wife and mother.

Chronic illness

With a short-term illness or an injury, everyone focuses on getting the patient well as quickly as possible. With chronic conditions—that is, long-term illnesses with no known cure—the emphasis must be on vigilant care and treatment that will promote the quality and fullness of life. There is no blueprint for this, since each person has a unique personality and different needs. But there is no doubt that maintaining meaningful relationships and contacts with the community, as well as developing personal interests, provides the affected person with a greater sense of self-value and overall enjoyment of life.

WHEN TO TAKE A BREAK

If you are looking after someone with a long-term illness or disability, much of your time will be spent on tiring and demanding tasks, such as bathing, dressing, or lifting the person, cooking special meals, possibly feeding them, keeping them company, and generally being responsible for everything. However much you love the person you are caring for, strain is inevitable, and may become critical. Unlike other employees, carers seldom get automatic breaks or holidays, but this does not mean you need them less, or are less entitled to take them. In fact, breaks are essential if you are to continue caring effectively.

Warning signs

Carers often expect too much of themselves, and you may feel guilty that you are not doing enough, or doing everything wrong, or even that it is not you who is ill but someone else. Remember, you must look after yourself first to be able to care for someone else. Learn to recognize when you are overtired or under too much stress. Ask yourself the following questions:
• Am I losing my temper frequently?
• Am I sleeping badly for no obvious reason?
• Do I feel tired all the time?
• Am I constantly tearful?
• Have small things that didn't bother me before become too much to bear?

Organizing a break

If you find yourself exhausted, do not hesitate to ask for help or for "time off." You could probably start by asking other relatives to visit; sometimes, company is all you need to lift your spirits.

Some official bodies and charities also run relief schemes; their services usually range from providing someone to sit in for a couple of hours to moving the patient to a residential home temporarily so you can take a proper holiday.

Dealing with bitterness

Although we may easily recognize that bitterness is destructive, it is still hard to fight against if you or a loved one has been struck down with an illness that affects your ability to live the life you would like. Finding ways to avoid succumbing to bitterness,

while recognizing that it will probably resurface at times, is essential. Accepting that the problem will not go away, and understanding the probable course of the illness, is important for both sufferers and carers. Recognize that, whatever your problem, you are seldom alone. For many chronic illnesses such as diabetes, Parkinson's disease, or multiple sclerosis, there are often support groups, charities, and self-help organizations that will help you to cope with the special problems you will face—providing both practical advice and contact with other people for emotional support. There are also books you can consult, and you should always turn to your doctor or a counselor if you feel you need to.

THE MIND UNDER PRESSURE

All of us are sometimes beset by ordinary problems that might preoccupy our minds or cause us to worry a great deal, and some of us are prone to behavior that may be quirky or eccentric but is not at all harmful. Beyond this, however, are mental disorders that may be more serious. Such conditions are marked by a prolonged pattern of behavior that causes a person distress and disability or impaired functioning in a significant area. For example, you may perform brilliantly at work but suffer from an eating disorder, or you may be welcoming to others in your own home, but suffer from an uncontrollable fear of going outside.

Types of disorder

Mental disorders range from phobias, anxiety, depression, eating problems, and alcohol and drug addiction, to more serious mental illnesses such as schizophrenia, which is often accompanied by extreme delusions and hallucinations. Any of these

Feeling fragile?
Chronic pressure or unhappiness can undermine your ability to cope with daily life, and may be a prelude to some type of behavioral disorder.

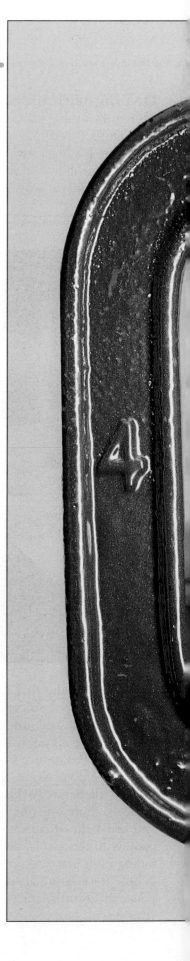

HELP IS AVAILABLE

Many people describe their depression as an emptiness within; some seek to fill this almost physical hollowness through addictive behavior.

If you have this problem, or are living with an alcoholic or someone who suffers from acute depression, what can you do?

• **Accept that you can only change yourself.** You cannot change another person, or hope that another person will change you.

• **Seek help.** Psychotherapy often helps to uncover the underlying causes of addictive behavior. Other treatments include cognitive therapy to challenge and change destructive thought patterns, and behavioral therapy, which introduces new rewards while inhibiting the destructive aspects of despair.

• **Consider medication.** To treat serious depression, some doctors and psychiatrists are likely to suggest a course of antidepressants. There are many types, and they are usually highly effective. For some types of addiction, notably heroin, methadone treatment may help. To treat severe anxiety, your doctor may consider tranquilizers helpful in the short term.

• **Join support groups.** It helps to know that you are not alone.

conditions indicates that a person has some sort of deep-seated problem or illness, with the result that he or she is less able to cope with the demands of daily living. The more extreme the disorder, the greater is the anguish suffered by the person and by his or her family members.

Thankfully, continuing research into mental illness has contributed to greater understanding, and more information is available. Increasingly, too, people who suffer from psychological disorders talk frankly about them as part of the healing process: Many a media or sports star has publicly discussed his or her addictive or self-destructive behavior. Even serious disorders, such as schizophrenia, can be controlled by medication and do not necessarily mean a lifetime of desolation.

Depression

The single most common mental disorder is depression. It ranges in severity from the transient "blues" that all of us occasionally suffer to feelings of intense loneliness and despair that can last for months or even years. It also affects people in different ways: Some struggle through their periods of darkness on their own—Winston Churchill, the great British statesman, described his periods of depression as his "black dog" but continued to work—while others need years of psychotherapy or repeated brief hospitalization. When depression alternates with extreme elation and hyperactivity, it is called manic depression or bipolar syndrome.

Acute self-hatred is a common feature of depression. Sufferers tend to blame themselves, not only for their condition, but for everything negative in their work or home environment. There are physical signs of depression, too, including loss of appetite, disrupted sleeping patterns, constant exhaustion, loss of libido, and difficulty in concentrating and making decisions. Depressed people feel apathetic, overcome by a hopelessness and inner deadness. At its worst, depression cuts the person off from the rest of the world, including those who are nearest and dearest to them. They stop communicating entirely, often avoiding people and staying in bed for long periods.

If you recognize these feelings or behavior in yourself, or in someone you know, do not hesitate to seek help immediately.

DEATH AND MOURNING

W E FEAR DEATH not because, like most crises, it is unpredictable, but because it is inevitable. Indeed, it is one of the few certainties of life. Yet it is something that most of us are unprepared for. The death of a loved one causes acute distress, often triggering a crisis in those left to mourn, affecting their relationships, work, health, and sense of their own identity. It can turn people's lives upside down, although, as with other crises, it may precipitate positive changes as well as causing pain.

Sudden death and suicide

When someone dies unexpectedly—in an accident or from a sudden heart attack—family and close friends are catapulted from their "normal," predictable existence into emotional chaos. As well as shock and grief, there may be aching remorse, largely due to unresolved conflicts or unexpressed feelings of love and gratitude. The death also affects the mourners' view of the world: Suddenly, nothing can be relied upon or taken for granted, and the world seems fraught with danger, especially if the death occurred as a result of an accident. In response, bereaved people may sometimes become accident-prone or unconsciously careless about their own safety or well-being. In time, however, people can recover a sense of trust in the world.

The effects of a suicide are always devastating, but bereavement may be complicated by more intense feelings of anger and guilt. Even if there is a suicide note, those who mourn ask themselves, "Why? Why didn't I realize he was so desperate? Why didn't he come to me? Maybe I could have stopped him." The guilt and self-blame can be so acute that the process of mourning is impeded, and the bereaved may for a long time only be able to think of the dead person with pain, rather than with sadness and fondness for the good times they shared together. Specialist suicide counseling can be very helpful.

Shattered life

The impact of the sudden death of someone you love often shatters your sense of security, leaving you feeling fragile.

Enclosed in grief

When you are grieving, you can feel shut off from the rest of the world, even from those you love most. The support of friends and family can help you through the most painful times.

Death of a child

The loss of a child involves the most acute grief. As well as anguish, there is an overwhelming sense that it is unnatural and unjust for a child to die before its parents. Bereaved parents are likely to feel intense anger at the world and whoever or whatever is seen to be the cause of the death. The loss inevitably affects the rest of the family: Surviving siblings may feel guilty just for being alive, or the parents separate because they remind each other of their loss. Support from other bereaved parents is invaluable.

Accepting grief

If the deceased has suffered a long illness, mourners may be comforted by knowing that the person's suffering is over. When an elderly person dies, a family can usually recognize and accept that death is a normal and inevitable part of the cycle of life.

When one family member dies, the others may become closer, united in their grief and the realization that they should enjoy their relationships to the full. In some cases, however, family members express their grief through anger at each other, or they may withdraw from each other out of self-protection: Fearful of unbearable loss, they conclude that it is safer not to care for or about people.

The process of grieving—of talking, weeping, remembering—helps bereaved people reach the point where they can accept their loss, yet remember the person they loved with pleasure as well as sadness (see "Stages of Grief," pp. 52-53). Death and mourning help us also to understand that life is precious and should not be wasted. Remembering this can help us to gain strength from difficult times.

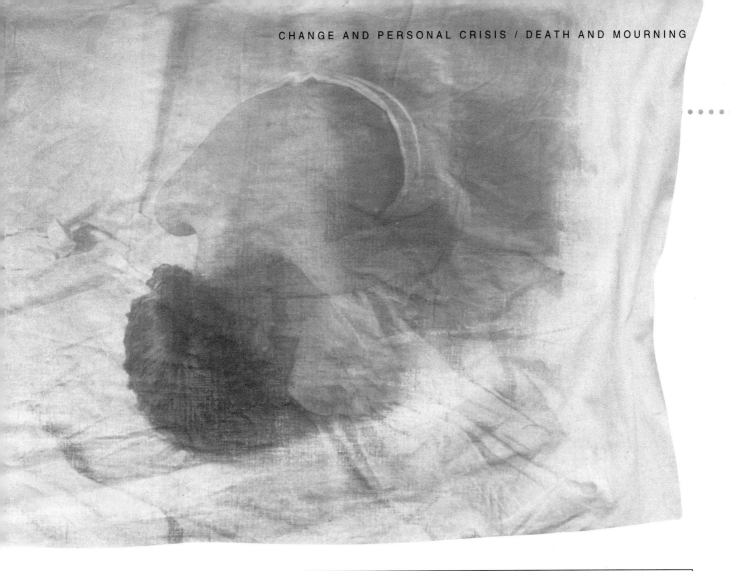

BEREAVED CHILDREN

Coping with the death of someone close can be particularly difficult for children, especially if the adults around them are absorbed in their own grief. Bereaved children may withdraw and become very quiet; because they appear "calm," they may not be given the support they need.

Children often first encounter death through television, so they may associate it with violence and feel alarmed when a family member dies. The disruption of routine and a feeling of instability can also make children feel insecure and threatened.

Just as adults may experience mood swings after a bereavement—which can be alarming and confusing—children may act out of character or behave oddly. These guidelines may help:

• Do not try to shield children from the realities of death by being euphemistic. Saying that the dead person has "gone away" or "gone to a better place" may confuse children, and they may wonder why the person no longer seems to want to see them.

• Encourage the child to focus on the good memories of the person and the things they did together, and on any talents or qualities that the child has in common with them. This helps them understand how people can live on in our thoughts, feelings, and memories, and gives them a sense of the continuity of life.

• Children may feel overwhelmed by the intensity of their feelings. Encourage them to express them—including those that may feel unacceptable, such as anger. If suppressed, feelings are merely rechanneled and may surface in problem behavior, eating or sleeping difficulties, or psychosomatic illness.

• Do let children attend the funeral if they want to. Although it may be upsetting, it is an important part of the process of accepting that someone is gone.

STAGES OF GRIEF

Suffering the death of a loved one, or any other loss, is often regarded as something we have to "get over," as if grief were an obstacle to be overcome, or an experience to be forgotten and put behind us as soon as possible. This approach is rarely helpful, however. Grieving, and coming to terms with a loss, is not about forgetting what's happened; nor is it about being "strong" and denying or refusing to talk about your feelings of loss.

The process of grieving, which can be long and painful, is an essential one, and there are really no short cuts that allow you to avoid all your sadness and emotional pain. Going through the stages of grief helps you learn to accept and integrate the loss into your life, so that you can look back with pleasure on your memories, while focusing your energies on your present and your future.

Shifting feelings

A loss may be of many kinds: It may be the death of someone close, an illness affecting a loved one or yourself, a divorce, the realization that a long-held dream may be out of reach, or even the loss of a treasured possession. Your feelings about it may pass through a number of stages, some of which will overlap. These transitions and shifts are normal, but they may feel confusing and disturbing. To feel sad one minute, then suddenly angry and irritable for no obvious reason, is unsettling, and you may feel unstable and alarmed.

Anger

When any sort of significant loss has turned your life upside down, it is natural to feel angry. This anger may be expressed in outbursts or flare-ups toward other people, including close family and friends, and even strangers such as shop assistants. It may also manifest itself as bitterness, which makes you touchy and difficult to be around. Anger is quite often directed inward and may become part of the pain of depression. Religious people may rail against their god for letting such a terrible thing happen to them.

Disbelief and denial

A common initial response to loss is disbelief. In some ways, this is a self-protective measure: It allows us to absorb the new information slowly, rather than take it on board all at once when it might be overwhelming and affect our stability. If this denial stage continues for a long time, however, it can prevent us from moving on. While it can be a way of trying to keep painful recognition at bay, feelings will inevitably resurface in other ways—for example, in aggressive behavior toward others or in psychosomatic illness.

Up from the depths
The process of grieving over a serious loss involves a number of recognizable stages; you may pass through some or all of them before you move beyond the pain to feeling more positive and hopeful.

Guilt

If someone has died, you may feel guilt even if you had a good relationship with the deceased and have nothing for which you could rationally blame yourself. Death is so major an event that all your feelings are overwhelming. Graham, for example, felt responsible for his wife's death in a car crash because he had encouraged her to learn to drive.

A sense of guilt also stems from realizing that it is too late to right any wrongs or tell the person how you felt about them.

Sadness and depression

If you are sad or depressed, it can seem as if you will never be happy again, but these feelings are a very natural stage of grief, and it is vital to accept them—painful though they are—rather than trying to suppress them. If you have lost someone close to you, it inevitably leaves a hole in your life. Loss *is* painful, but remind yourself that this pain does ease with time and that you have the strength to experience your feelings as they really are.

Relatives and friends may try to distract you to stop you crying or avoid talking about your loss in the mistaken belief that you will forget if no-one mentions it and you don't talk about it. Although well-meant, this slows down the healing process. Bereaved people need to talk about their feelings—perhaps to a good friend or relative, or to a specialist bereavement counselor. If someone you know has suffered a loss, you can always say: "I'm here for you if you want to talk, but if you'd rather not, then I understand." This allows grieving people to choose, rather than feeling either that they can't "impose" or that they have to talk even if they don't feel like it.

Coming through

When you have finally accepted your loss and can see hope in your life again, you have come through the grieving process. In the case of a death, this doesn't mean that you have forgotten the person or that you no longer care. Any loss continues to live on in your memory and feelings, but this should not hold you back or prevent you from planning a future or forming new emotional attachments.

There is no set period of time for grieving: It takes as long as it takes, and no two people are alike, so be patient with yourself. Don't berate yourself by thinking "I ought to be over this by now" or let anyone else put pressure on you. Give yourself permission to feel whatever comes up; it is only by doing this that you will be able to integrate the loss so that it does not dominate your life, and you can move on to a brighter future.

COPING WITH CRIME

MINOR INCIDENTS of crime are now, sadly, a part of life. This is particularly so in urban areas, where your car may be broken into, unguarded possessions at the leisure center may go missing, or you may be the target of a pickpocket. Even if you have not been the victim of such crimes yourself, someone close to you probably has. While most such events will not be unduly serious or traumatic, you will still need to get over the immediate shock, and deal with the feelings you may experience.

Can you fight back?

Early one evening, while it was still light, Maureen got off the train in her busy suburb, walked to the automatic cash machine, withdrew some money, and carefully put it away in her handbag. Suddenly, a man appeared, grabbed her handbag, and ran off.

Maureen was too shocked to react, and was able to move only when a passer-by asked if she was all right. The passer-by

The aftermath of crime
If you have been mugged or your house has been burgled, your fear may make you feel like a prisoner in your own home. Take steps to overcome your fear and claim your life back.

helped her to call the police, and an officer then drove her around looking for the mugger and her handbag. But she had not really seen him, and the police could not satisfactorily proceed without an identification.

Maureen felt extremely angry with her attacker, but subsequently also felt very jumpy when anyone walked down the street behind her. Some of her friends thought that she was overreacting. After all, it had happened so quickly, and she had not been harmed. Only when she went to a victim support group for help did Maureen discover that she was not overreacting; she also stopped feeling so angry, and realized that she was not a coward because she had been unable

HELP YOURSELF RECOVER

• Take advantage of any help the police can offer; they should be able to give you practical advice on how best to protect yourself and your home.
• Ensure that any stolen credit and debit cards are cancelled immediately. If you feel too shaky to do this, you might ask someone else for help, but taking practical steps can help you feel more in charge.
• Don't take it personally; you were probably a random victim rather than singled out.

Be secure
Taking practical, preventive steps, such as fitting a door chain or an alarm, can help you feel like less of a victim.

The criminal is not interested in who you are but in what you own. He or she would probably not want to meet you again—and in most cases would not recognize you.

to fight back. Gradually her anger and anxiety lessened, and her confidence grew so that she was once again able to go out alone. The group encouraged her to join a self-defense class, and a welcome side-effect was greater fitness.

Reactions to crime

As a victim of crime, you have to cope with a temporary crisis. How much you are affected will depend on your ability to cope with crisis and anxiety generally. Everyone responds differently.

The seriousness of the crime will affect how you react. Car crime may simply be irritating, but even if it results in something as minor as a broken window, it costs time and money, often contributes to increased insurance premiums, and causes great inconvenience—all of which can leave you feeling resentful and under pressure.

Mugging is usually far more traumatic, and produces a wide range of feelings. A young male victim may feel angry and also inadequate because he failed to

protect himself, and may want to search for his attacker. An elderly woman, however, may experience increased anxiety about her personal safety, yet receive greater support from friends, family, and the authorities because she is perceived as needing greater protection.

Safe at home

People consider their homes as sacrosanct places where they should feel safe. Because burglary is an invasion of that safety and a violation of your privacy, it is thus particularly hard to come to terms with. You may miss your television or computer, but may also lose items of great sentimental value. You may also feel physically threatened, so it helps to remember that burglars usually call while you're out.

You may also feel frustrated that the police can do very little, and be tempted to take action yourself. This is never advisable. Instead, use the action list on these pages to help you recover from your experience and get your life back to normal.

- Talk about your experience to someone who will allow you to express your feelings without censure, perhaps your partner, a close friend, or a counselor.
- Take advantage of any professional help, or join a victim support group.
- Reduce the chance of crime by improving your home security, and by joining a self-defense class.

- Accept that it may take some time for you to feel safe again. Try not to rush into dramatic responses, such as moving house or purchasing a weapon, if you have been burgled or attacked.
- Once you have fully recovered, consider helping others through neighborhood watch schemes or victim support groups.
- Remember, you have done nothing wrong: Crime is never the fault of the victim.

ASSAULT

The fear of being assaulted is much greater than the chances of actually being attacked. Elderly women fear assault most, but are least likely to be attacked; young men, who are the most common victims, worry about it least. Also, people are more likely to be assaulted by someone they know than by a stranger.

Whatever the circumstances, the effects of a physical attack can be devastating. Understanding what sort of feelings you may have to confront, and how to cope with them, will give you a much better chance of recovering, and of regaining your confidence and sense of security.

Sexual assault

For many women, the possibility of rape is too awful to contemplate. Many do not report sexual assaults to the police. If they do, as recent "date rape" cases have shown, it can be hard to prove the incident occurred, and the victim often feels blamed for what happened. Men may also be victims of rape.

A serious sexual assault has both physical and psychological consequences. Immediately after the attack, the victim is most vulnerable, perhaps in physical pain and emotional shock. Having a close friend or partner around is a vital support and can help the victim report the incident to the police. You may desperately want to wash yourself, but must wait until forensic tests have been done, if any subsequent prosecution is to succeed.

Even if there has been no physical injury, you should see a doctor. Do not feel that you cannot ask for help, especially since the psychological impact of any attack cannot be underestimated. Most people feel shock, fear, guilt, and humiliation. You may try to stop thinking and talking about the assault, but it is important to express your feelings.

A close friend or relative may provide support, but trained counselors know best how to help you recover. If you have a partner, he or she may find it difficult to be supportive, and may also benefit from accompanying you to see a counselor.

HOW TO BE STREETWISE

Evaluate the situation
Are you leaving work late, or after dark, or going to or through unfamiliar places? Would it be best to take a taxi, or to telephone someone and arrange to be met? Think about situations in advance. Don't take safety for granted.

Know where to walk
Avoid areas that are poorly lit or sparsely populated. Walk in the middle of the sidewalk and face oncoming traffic. Cross the road if you suspect you are being followed. Don't stop walking if someone speaks to you.

Look confident
Body language can help you avoid trouble, so "walk tall" and keep your hands out of your pockets. Walk briskly, and look like you know exactly where you're going. Carry your bag in front of you close to your body.

Physical assault

Although men are more likely than women to be victims of violent physical attack, there are many situations that affect both. Simply belonging to one group of friends may lead to confrontation with a rival group: This can occur if you look different, or belong to a different social or racial group, or support the "wrong" sports team. You may get caught up in a violent event such as an armed robbery or public disorder. In all cases, even if you are not physically injured, you will probably be shocked and frightened, and may feel vulnerable and panicky later on. Even if you think you are not affected, do look for support and accept offers of counseling: If the police become involved in any incident, such services may be provided.

While you can avoid dark alleyways or dangerous districts, and learn self-defense, assault can happen to anyone. Always remember that it is not your fault. Realizing that you were not to blame is the first and most important step toward recovery.

Out of control
If you are assaulted, the memory of the event can dominate your thoughts.

Be vigilant
Scan the area ahead and around for signs of trouble. Headphones make it hard to hear cars or people coming from behind you. Never have your back to potential danger: If you hear a noise, turn and find out what is happening.

Conceal your valuables
Expensive jewelry or watches are invitations to a mugger, so if you're wearing any, cover them up. Divide cash and credit cards, and put them into different or inside pockets. Wear a body wallet under your clothes.

Call for help
If someone threatens you, walk quickly or run to the nearest house or busy area. Don't ignore anything you think *might* be dangerous. Assume it is. If you think you are in real danger, scream for help.

GROUP TRAUMA

BEHIND THE HEADLINES about automobile pile-ups, earthquakes, bombs, and other violent tragedies are the many people who have to overcome one of the most difficult experiences of their lives. Those involved have to contend with a crisis of enormous proportions: Their lives may have been threatened, causing immeasurable stress. They may feel that the whole structure of their lives has vanished, and that they may never recover.

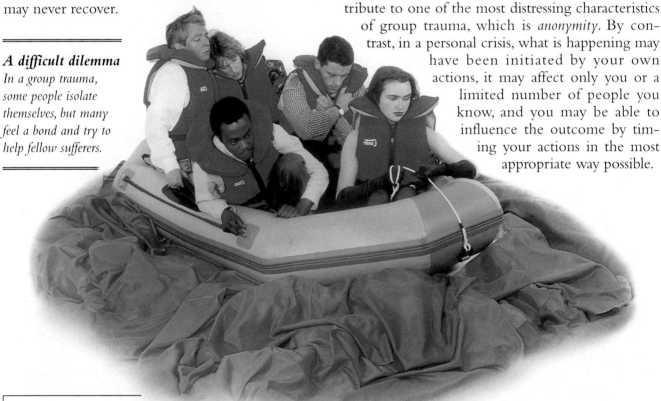

A difficult dilemma
In a group trauma,
some people isolate
themselves, but many
feel a bond and try to
help fellow sufferers.

Characteristics of group trauma

When a large number of people are injured or killed, many more than those directly involved are affected. In an airplane or train crash, for instance, the passengers—whether they are physically injured or not—are not the only ones to suffer from trauma: so do their friends and relatives, the people living nearby, the emergency services, and the general public. The sheer numbers of people involved contribute to one of the most distressing characteristics of group trauma, which is *anonymity*. By contrast, in a personal crisis, what is happening may have been initiated by your own actions, it may affect only you or a limited number of people you know, and you may be able to influence the outcome by timing your actions in the most appropriate way possible.

CASE HISTORY

Steven decided he would work for the Red Cross when he was 18 years old, after having witnessed a middle-aged man have a heart attack on the street: "I couldn't do anything for him, and I never wanted to feel so helpless again."

Despite years of training and experience, however, Steven and four colleagues had to face the fact that they couldn't save everyone when three out of five people in a two-car accident died. "What saved us all from despair," he said, "was that we trusted each other's ability and knew we had tried."

In a group trauma, however, your identity—who you are and how you expect to cope—is completely overwhelmed by the scale and unpredictability of the event, and the fact that many of those involved have been "thrown together." Most do not even know each other.

Anonymity is coupled with the another troubling dimension of group trauma, which is *chance*. The apparent randomness of a disaster often results in a painfully bewildering sense of inadequacy, and the aftermath of a group trauma is often marked by repeated re-thinking of the event as people ask themselves if they could have made a different decision—taken a different plane, for instance.

Coping with feelings

A wide range of feelings is likely to affect both the victims of a group trauma and also those who help them. Members of the emergency or rescue services, such as police officers and paramedics, frequently have access to counselors and stress management courses, or they may have been trained in advance to cope with specific events. They also develop their own ways of coping—such as by using humor—that can help them.

Others, however—people who are not professional helpers, for instance, or passers-by who become rescuers—may have less idea of the reactions that might occur.

• Insecurity and anxiety are common. People who had thought that their lives were orderly and predictable may become acutely aware of their own vulnerability, and suffer for a long time from the feeling that tragedy may strike at any time.

• Guilt may affect people who have survived a tragedy where others have died. Some do not understand why they lived, and may become obsessed with the idea that they should have done something to avert or alleviate the trauma.

• Flashbacks, nightmares, or obsessional thoughts may occur after the event, so that people are forced to relive the trauma again and again.

• The need to escape terrifying fears may lead some survivors to abuse alcohol or drugs.

• Severe depression may affect survivors of a group trauma—they may feel "low" or miserable, or that their lives are "unreal." As a result, they may be unable to make decisions or to eat properly. In a profound sense, they feel that their lives have come to a complete standstill, that they are "stuck," and it becomes difficult to re-integrate themselves into their former lives, or to plan for the future.

Re-thinking

As uncomfortable as these feelings are, they nonetheless stimulate many people to reconsider their lives, and many are grateful for the chance to recommit themselves to the values that they consider most important.

If you or someone you know has been involved in a traumatic incident, you may have to ask for help and support from your family, friends, or doctor. Do not hesitate to do so.

No protection
One of the after-effects of suffering a trauma is that you feel vulnerable and exposed.

HOW TO HELP

An effective strategy for recovering from group trauma should involve these steps—the "5Rs":

• **Removal.** The person should be removed from the scene of the incident as soon as possible.

• **Rest.** Following any severe physical or psychological trauma, people need time to recover from the effects of stress and fear.

• **Recounting.** Someone who has been through a major trauma should be encouraged to talk about it as much as possible, and should never be told that they should put the experience to the back of their minds. Even if they succeed in doing this, in the long term there may be psychological or psychosomatic reactions (see "Post-Traumatic Stress," pp. 60-61).

• **Reassurance.** People who may be suffering from survival guilt need to know that they have a right to live their lives, and that they are not responsible for someone else's injuries or death. They need to feel that they did everything they possibly could, and are not cowards or failures.

• **Recovery and return.** People vary greatly in how long they take to recover and in their ability to cope with trauma, and should be allowed to set their own pace.

POST-TRAUMATIC STRESS

I F YOU HAVE BEEN INVOLVED IN—or even simply witnessed—anything from a minor accident to a major disaster, you will probably experience stress for a few days or weeks after the event, and then expect life to return to normal. Some people, however, experience distressing and disabling symptoms for much longer, occasionally for many years.

Whatever the crisis, your friends, family members, and work colleagues may have offered sympathy and practical assistance. Despite these reassurances, however, you may suffer from sleeplessness, nightmares, panic attacks, weepiness, and feelings of futility or guilt about what you did or did not do during the event. If these symptoms persist or intensify for more than eight weeks, you may be suffering from post-traumatic stress disorder (PTSD). Even soldiers or police officers, who are trained and are usually able to deal effectively with unexpected events, accidents, or life-threatening disasters, may suffer similar delayed reactions.

Talking prevents prolonged stress

Researchers have found that a procedure known as "debriefing" can alleviate—and sometimes even prevent—symptoms of PTSD. Debriefing is primarily a "talking cure" in which survivors, helpers, or witnesses of a crisis review how they felt or acted during or after a traumatic incident. Debriefing usually occurs in a group context, but even one-to-one support—perhaps from an insightful friend or member of the family—can be helpful.

One of the great benefits of debriefing is the reassurance that many symptoms and reactions are very "normal" responses to abnormal events. A debriefing group does not encourage false optimism, but does allow people to express their feelings freely and in complete confidence. Participants often find that, once they acknowledge their feelings, they can mobilize their strength and devise their own strategies for recovery.

A place of safety
After a traumatic event, people need to unburden themselves of intense or frightening feelings in an atmosphere of complete trust and confidence. This may be easiest to do with fellow survivors.

REBUILDING TAKES TIME

In an attempt to re-establish predictability in their lives, many people desperately want to return to their former activities. This need to restore what may well be an idealized past can be a flight from present pain or guilt, feelings that often accompany major trauma. Others, however, need to create new patterns, and radically change their career goals or relationships.

Although they appear to be motivated by "second-chance" optimism, many survivors find it very difficult to trust that the world is predictable. They often expect disaster to disrupt the fragile security of their re-established lives, and frequently are overwhelmed with feelings of futility.

The sword of Damocles

One study of adults who had survived childhood cancer described them as feeling like Damocles, a figure from Greek mythology who was made to sit through a feast with a sword suspended over his head by a single hair. In this way, he was forced to learn about the insecurity of happiness.

Many survivors of life-threatening illnesses or accidents live with this sense of fragility. The same feeling, however, can engender a belief that life is too precious to waste, and simple pleasures—sharing joyful family occasions, making time for creative pursuits—take on new importance.

Go at your own pace

Perhaps the most important thing for survivors to remember is that every recovery is unpredictable: It takes time, and there are no set schedules or ready-made answers. Trauma may affect many people, such as when soldiers fight in a war zone, but each individual's recovery from the crisis will be different from anyone else's.

Brian Keenan, who was held as a hostage in Lebanon for four-and-a-half years, wrote that recovery is "a slow process of rediscovery, where denial or flight from the inward turmoil is the antithesis of self-healing…" He added, "We may be helped but we cannot be pushed or misdirected."

When to seek help

The following warning signs will help you decide if you, or someone you know, is suffering from PTSD. If so, talking to an experienced counselor is advisable.

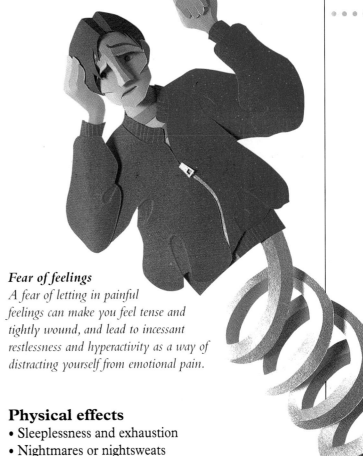

Fear of feelings
A fear of letting in painful feelings can make you feel tense and tightly wound, and lead to incessant restlessness and hyperactivity as a way of distracting yourself from emotional pain.

Physical effects
- Sleeplessness and exhaustion
- Nightmares or nightsweats
- Inability to eat
- Increased smoking or drinking
- Hyper-reactivity to stimuli, such as an extreme startle response, and trembling
- Hyperactivity (always needing to keep busy to avoid feelings)

Feelings
- Loss of self-esteem
- Loss of purpose and aim
- Intense loneliness and lack of trust
- Guilt and self-hatred
- Constantly feeling vulnerable

Behavior
- Inability to make decisions
- Irritability and sudden, unpredictable outbursts of aggression or violence
- Impulsive or "out of character" actions, such as shoplifting or reckless spending
- Retreating into isolation
- Problems with relationships.

CHAPTER THREE

GOOD NEWS CRISES

IT'S TEMPTING TO THINK that joyful events in our lives—whether it's getting married, having a baby, or starting a new job—will be completely positive and fulfilling, but this is rarely the case. Good news can often bring a crisis in its wake. Any significant change—even one you have initiated yourself—is also inherently stressful because it forces you to let go of the comfortable, familiar patterns of the past, and to adjust to what may be an entirely new set of circumstances.

When the sound of wedding bells has faded, married life may not always be the rosy bliss you imagined. "Marriage," pages 64-65, looks at the feelings that frequently affect newlyweds, such as post-honeymoon blues, when the prosaic concerns of everyday life seem a dreary anti-climax after the excitement of the wedding. In order to forge a rewarding and fulfilling relationship, it's important to have realistic expectations, to take responsibility for your own happiness, to be willing to share, and to work together to plan your future.

Having a baby can be the most miraculous and joyous event in a person's life, but new parents may also feel overwhelmed by the demands of a helpless, crying infant, as well as the prospect of a lifelong responsibility. A father may also struggle with jealousy as the baby takes his place as the primary focus of his partner's concern. Being aware of possible problems, and enlisting help from family and friends, can minimize difficulties (see "Becoming a Parent," pp. 66-67).

You may also look forward to moving house, but find yourself unexpectedly anxious about the process. As well as all the practical demands—negotiating, packing, organizing, and so forth—the upheaval and the break in continuity can undermine your sense of stability and security. Being well-prepared and organized will help keep stress to a minimum (see "Moving House," pp. 68-69).

An important part of your sense of identity may depend on what you do for a living, so it's not surprising that an exciting major change in your work life, such as starting a new job (pp. 70-71), changing your career (pp. 72-73), or facing retirement (pp. 74-75) can also be very unsettling. Being aware of the problems of a major change does not take away from the benefits: You will be able to refocus on what you really want, redirect your energies, reclaim interests you had abandoned, and expand your interests and capabilities in new directions.

EVEN THE BEST NEWS, SUCH AS WINNING THE LOTTERY, MAY BRING ABOUT A CRISIS. A FRESH START MAY BE POSITIVE, BUT WILL ALSO AFFECT YOUR SELF-IMAGE, EXPECTATIONS, AND RELATIONSHIPS IN UNEXPECTED WAYS.

MARRIAGE

COMMITTING yourself to a long-term relationship by getting married or by moving in together should be one of the high points of anyone's life. For many people, however, it creates such high expectations—of a perfect life together, of never arguing, of getting it "right"—that inevitably they become disappointed and disillusioned. The truth is that no relationship is perfect all the time because it inherently involves difficulties and misunderstandings that require insight, flexibility, and patience to resolve. It is not surprising that you will occasionally feel let down, but making such a commitment, and deciding to share your life with someone, will bring great benefits.

BUILD A PARTNERSHIP

Establishing a serious, committed relationship is not easy, but a strong alliance will help you work through any bad patches together. These guidelines will help you create a close partnership without becoming too dependent or smothering each other.

Forge a strong alliance
• Create a sense of a future together. Plan shared goals and changes in your lives, such as starting a family, decorating your home, moving to a new location, or learning a new language.

Shared lives
You and your partner will be happier to share if you do not become too entwined and can still retain a sense of being separate individuals.

Show love and support

• Give your partner your full loyalty and moral support, especially when he or she is having a difficult time.
• Take each other's goals and achievements seriously, and be sympathetic and constructive—rather than indifferent and critical—about each other's disappointments.
• Show your affection for each other. Don't assume your partner knows how you feel just because you're together.
• Recognize each other's individuality, and the need to have time and space apart. This is not a rejection of the other person: You will enjoy each other's company more if you know you are together by choice rather than habit.

Be flexible

• Find things you both enjoy that you can do together—and don't make these activities a focus of competition or rivalry.
• Take time out from the shared routine of everyday life, which may become monotonous for you both. Get away from your everyday environment, perhaps simply going somewhere new for the day together.
• Be flexible in your roles. Sometimes, one of you may have to be the more caring partner. No-one can—or should be—the "strong" one all the time. Allow yourselves room to grow.

No more "rose-colored glasses"

Getting married or living together can sometimes create problems in a relationship that was previously happy. There are various reasons, including:
• *Adjusting to living together.* You have to work out a practical routine that suits both of you.
• *A sense of anti-climax.* Partners may feel resentment when their expectations aren't met or when the initial romance is clouded by practical concerns, particularly when you have to face the banalities of everyday life after an idyllic honeymoon.
• *Feeling panicky.* People may have sudden doubts about making such a major commitment.
• *Feeling engulfed.* Suddenly being in each other's company day after day can seem claustrophobic, leaving you with little time or space to yourself.

None of these factors means that you made a mistake; these worries usually right themselves in time, but they should not be ignored. Discuss how you could improve problem areas. Difficulties are much less likely to precipitate a crisis if you have appropriate expectations of a relationship: Your cherished illusions may be challenged, but you can build a relationship based on who you really are.

Facing reality and adjusting to change

Being realistic doesn't mean being pessimistic, but it does mean not expecting your partner to be the sole source of your happiness and fulfillment, or to assume that his or her primary concern should be looking after and pleasing you. A good relationship should enhance your life and all your other goals, rather than be your sole aim.

Flexibility and adaptability are your greatest allies in a relationship. If you previously lived alone and quite independently, you probably will have to make many compromises. This can be difficult, and you may resent it even if you consciously know that it is only right to consult your partner over decisions. If your fundamental values are basically the same, it is easier to accept differences of opinion over minor issues, but you may have to work harder to resolve conflicts about more highly charged issues: childrearing, career priorities, money, and household routines. Living with someone else also demands tolerance and the ability to negotiate. Being prepared to talk and compromise, rather than feeling you must "win" at any cost, is vital if your relationship is to succeed in the long term.

BECOMING A PARENT

Becoming a parent is a major turning point in a person's life. For the mother, the obvious physical changes are matched by equally strong inner emotional changes. For the father, the experience of losing a close, intimate twosome and exchanging it for a noisy threesome requires an enormous adjustment. No matter how many books you read, how many of your friends you talk to, or how ready you think you are to start a family, you will still probably feel relatively unprepared for the experience when it happens.

Coping with needs

Having a child will bring to the surface many of the parents' own feelings about having been children themselves. If they are emotionally immature, they may find it difficult to cope with a tiny, demanding, helpless human being. This can spark off intense feelings of anger, which can be frightening. Susan, for example, was an adopted child who found giving birth a profoundly moving experience. Like most mothers, she had to confront the anxieties that frequently accompany the bliss and joy of parenthood; what she hadn't anticipated, however, were the feelings of jealousy and anger that her new baby aroused in her. These emotions stemmed from deep inside Susan—from the small, adopted child who had suffered great loss and pain.

"Baby blues"

No matter how much a woman may want to have a baby, she may have mixed feelings once it is born. Within a month after the birth, more than half of all new mothers experience some degree of postnatal depression. Many are tearful for a few hours, or feel "blue" for a few weeks, but some become more seriously depressed, and may require counseling.

This depression is principally due to the fact that the hormones that sustained the pregnancy and stimulated labor must find a new level, and as these hormones adjust, mood swings frequently occur. If a mother is suffering from a lack of sleep and chronic exhaustion, this will also contribute to her feeling that she cannot possibly cope.

A whole unit
The bond between a mother and her baby can be so intense that the father may feel excluded and neglected, but his support and involvement is important to both mother and child and to help establish their sense of being a family together.

Facing reality

Sometimes the degree of depression is related to how much the mother idealized the birth and the baby beforehand. It is quite common for mothers to have fantasies about their unborn child: They give the child a name, talk to him or her, and imagine what he or she will be like. If the woman is lonely and depressed, having a baby may seem like the way out of despair, but once the baby is born, and the enormous task of caring for a dependent and demanding infant becomes apparent, a woman's depression may deepen.

If you become depressed, you will probably find talking about your feelings and worries helpful, and you could ask a woman who is experienced with children—your mother, sister, or a friend—to help with the baby; they will probably be happy to reassure you. Sometimes, you may feel depressed simply because you are lonely, but if your depression persists or deepens, you should see your doctor. Only rarely is postnatal depression serious enough to require psychiatric treatment.

Re-establishing your identity

Even if you intend to go back to work, there is usually a period when you are at home alone with your new infant, and you may feel isolated, bored, frustrated, and resentful at the lack of adult company. How can you deal with these feelings?

• Ask for help with childcare. As soon as your baby will feed from a bottle, arrange for time to be "yourself." You might take it in turns with a friend to look after each other's child. Perhaps you could have an evening alone with your partner one week, and an evening with your friends the next.

• Don't feel guilty if you find you need to have some time alone. Dr. Miriam Stoppard, author of *Everywoman's Lifeguide*, suggests that every woman—especially a new mother—should have a day and time that the family accepts is her free time. You may want to take a walk, go to a museum, pursue your hobby, or have your hair done. The point is that this time is a recognized part of the family routine, and you have something to look forward to.

• Don't forget to make time for your partner. Even if you're both happy to share the responsibility of childcare, a good, stable relationship between the two of you is the best foundation for establishing a harmonious family life.

Dual roles

With each stage of a child's development, parents must adapt not only to the child but also to each other. The woman's role is both mother and wife, while the man's is father as well as husband. The stress involved in playing dual roles, and of switching

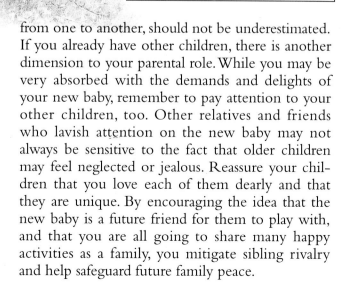

WHAT ABOUT FATHER?

In the weeks after birth, when the mother devotes herself to her baby, a father may feel dejected or unwanted. Yet it is often he who keeps the mother "sane" when childcare is tough. Even talking to the mother while the baby is asleep can give her the vital psychological "nourishment" she needs. For a mother to hear a baby crying in distress without knowing what is wrong can be very upsetting. If she feels inept and useless, she may panic and lose confidence. In addition to helping care for the baby, the father plays an important role in caring for and reassuring the mother, particularly in these difficult times. It is for this reason that single parenting is so difficult: There is no-one for the lone parent to lean on in times of distress.

from one to another, should not be underestimated. If you already have other children, there is another dimension to your parental role. While you may be very absorbed with the demands and delights of your new baby, remember to pay attention to your other children, too. Other relatives and friends who lavish attention on the new baby may not always be sensitive to the fact that older children may feel neglected or jealous. Reassure your children that you love each of them dearly and that they are unique. By encouraging the idea that the new baby is a future friend for them to play with, and that you are all going to share many happy activities as a family, you mitigate sibling rivalry and help safeguard future family peace.

MOVING HOUSE

MOVING HOUSE can be one of life's most stressful experiences. Your house or apartment is, after all, your home, and moving, even through choice, involves leaving behind what is familiar, safe, and comfortable to deal with the unknown. You may find it an exciting time, one that coincides with new opportunities or key transitions, such as a new job or a new baby. But such a big event can also cause anxiety, and it may be physically and mentally draining. However, to a certain degree, you can anticipate and learn how to minimize stress.

First of all, you need to be aware of the kind of factors that will produce stress, such as selling your old home, searching for your new home, arranging the finance, and coping with legal negotiations.

Even when you have successfully negotiated sale and purchase, the move itself can be stressful. Deciding on what to leave behind and what to pack, and where to put everything you've brought with you, is difficult and time-consuming. You may be leaving a home that has been the source of many happy memories for you and your family.

It's your move

Your first and most important consideration should be whether or not you can afford your new home. Buying a house out of your price range can land you in debt from which it is almost impossible to escape. Property is not always the sound investment it once was, and it is all too easy to underestimate the real costs. Take the time to work out, as far as possible, the expense involved, such as legal fees, surveys, and removal costs. Consider additional costs of relocation such as redecoration, new travel expenses, or increased household bills.

Don't just buy the first house you see that seems suitable, or make a hasty decision because you are fearful of losing your "dream home." Look at as many possible properties as you can. It will help you to make the right decision.

__Addressing the problem__
Moving house can involve a lot of paperwork and demands on your time, finances, and energy. Start a "house move" file so that all your documentation is kept together and you can find any papers easily.

KEYS TO STRESS CONTROL

By adopting a positive approach and a realistic attitude, you can deal with the disappointments, difficulties, and delays of moving house—and you may even enjoy the challenge.

• **Get your timing right.** Try to move when other factors in your life are stable, such as your job or relationships. Take enough time to make decisions.
• **Be realistic.** Assess your finances carefully and don't over-extend yourself. Don't expect everything to go like clockwork; be prepared for setbacks, and try to be patient.
• **Do your research.** Keep abreast of changes in the housing market, and look at the area you propose moving to. You will not just have a new house, but a new life, too—new neighbors, community, journeys, transport, shops, schools, and facilities.
• **Take control where you can.** Keep copies of all transactions. Use professionals, but remember that they work to your instructions. The better informed you are, the better service you will receive.
• **Book time off work.** You'll need it.
• **Ask for help from your partner, family, and friends.** Don't take it upon yourself to make all the decisions and practical arrangements.

Avoiding slip-ups
Moving house can generate unexpected problems as well as pleasures and benefits. With good preparation and a positive outlook, you can steer clear of slip-ups and enjoy the move.

Taking control

However carefully you plan, some elements of moving are out of your control, a fact that most people find unnerving. Once you have found a house you like and can afford, you are thrust into endless negotiations with bank managers, solicitors, estate agents, and your own prospective purchasers.

But you are not as helpless as you might think. By being positively involved, you can maintain a degree of control. Don't be afraid to ask questions. Keep notes of any queries as they arise, and make sure that anything you do not understand is fully explained by your professional advisers.

Your vendor may drop out suddenly, leaving you disappointed and angry. Rather than vent your frustrations on family and friends, start looking again right away. You may find the next house is a much better property than the one you lost.

If you already own a property, you need to make as much effort to sell it as to buy something else. It is usually better to have a definite purchaser before you make an offer on a new property.

Even if everything goes smoothly, change is unsettling, so give yourself time to adjust. Don't be surprised if you have a sense of anticlimax, regret, or disillusionment. You may miss the home and friends you left behind. Moving may seem to generate endless and overwhelming work, but re-establishing domestic routines and re-building your social life can soon restore your enthusiasm for this exhilarating and challenging time.

Don't forget about your children's feelings, especially if the move necessitates a change in school. Talk to them, explaining what is happening and why. Try to make it exciting and fun for them—and you might find it exciting and fun yourself.

STARTING A NEW JOB

OU FIND THE POSITION you want, do well at the interview, negotiate a good salary, and are offered the job. You read the letter, whoop for joy, and celebrate with friends and family. Suddenly, the euphoria fades and you are plagued with doubts.

You begin to wonder whether it will work out, whether you made promises you cannot fulfill. Maybe you exaggerated your experience and knowledge. You begin to think that you may hate the job, or worse, the people there may not like you. You may even wonder if the company is doing as well as you thought, and worry you could soon be unemployed again.

Relax—all these feelings are common, particularly for people who are newly promoted, returning to work after a period of unemployment, or embarking on a new career.

Under the spotlight
Most people starting a new job feel great pressure: They struggle to perform new tasks and to fit in with an existing group, and know their work is constantly being evaluated.

70

You're the one that they want

Remember that it was *you* your employers chose for the job, so they must be confident that you are the right person for their organization. Trust their ability to make that judgment—and trust your own judgment that, when you accepted the job, you believed you could do it, and wanted to.

The first week

The first few days in any new job are almost as important as the interview. Following these recommendations will help to ensure that you make a good first impression.

• Do as much research as you can before you start. You probably will have gathered a great deal of information before and during your interview, but you may be able to learn more from company reports and press cuttings (check your public library). You may have friends who know about the company. You can ask your new employer whether there is any other material that you could study to prepare for your new position.

• Dress appropriately so that you fit in. Ask your employer if there is a formal or expected dress code. You should get some idea about appropriate attire from your interview, but take note in your first week of whether you have chosen wisely—and adapt if you feel you haven't.

• When you meet the people you will be working with, be friendly and genuine. If you are to lead a group, it helps to say that you hope to get to know each of them, and to understand the contribution they are making to the organization. Briefly clarify the type of role you intend to play, and express your thanks for their support.

Either as a new manager or employee, you might consider saying that you have a great deal to learn but want to contribute. Your new colleagues may well be as nervous as you are, fearing that you will not fit in, or are the new broom brought in to sweep away established routines. If you are in a position to institute changes, make it clear to the staff that you will assess the situation carefully before doing so.

In your own time

When making decisions, think before you act so that you do not speak or act in haste. Deliberation will allow you to make a more considered response, and to present your opinion coherently and persuasively. It will also enable you to find out more about any factors that may have a bearing on your response. Faced with a demand for an instant decision, give yourself breathing space so you do not do something you may regret. You can always say, "Let me get back to you in an hour."

To be sure that you know exactly what is expected of you, and to evaluate your own progress, you might suggest to your employer that you meet regularly during the first months.

The most important thing to remember is that you shouldn't rush into action: You risk making errors of judgment based on insufficient knowledge. "Slow but sure" is better than setting a pace you cannot maintain.

Being a new employee can be a great advantage: You can look at the organization with fresh eyes, and your objectivity will contribute to your ability to make suggestions that may improve efficiency and raise morale. Bear in mind, however, that attempting to dictate policy will meet with resistance from your colleagues or employees. Bear in mind, too, that good relationships in the workplace are the key to a happy and successful working life.

CHANGING YOUR CAREER

Dissatisfaction with your current job, sudden unemployment, or early retirement might be the spur you need to help you embark on a new career path. You may be excited by the challenge, terrified by the potential pitfalls, or just doggedly determined to find a more fulfilling niche, but by carefully thinking things through and being well prepared you might find—or create—a much more rewarding occupation and lifestyle.

Go your own way
Working independently can be highly fulfilling and challenging, but you should be prepared for a great deal of independent decision-making, meticulous planning, and hours of hard work.

Getting on track

The hardest part of a career change is choosing the right direction rather than pursuing unsuitable or impossible aims on the spur of the moment. This is especially true if you have suddenly become unemployed, but taking stock is always important.

• Start by making two lists. On the first list, you should note all your talents, proven skills, and job experience. From this list, try to write an objective description of yourself as though you were looking at your qualifications for the first time. Make a second list that describes how you would like your life to be in ten years' time. Don't forget to consult your family or others who may be affected by your decisions.

• Using the list, try to think of at least four possible ways to achieve your aims. Start researching the career options you have listed.

• Go to the library and read as much as you can about each possibility. Also, read the appointments sections of any relevant professional or trade journals to see what sort of skills, experience, and qualifications are required.

COULD YOU GO IT ALONE?

If you can answer "Yes" to the questions below, starting your own business may suit you.

• Do you enjoy working on your own and can you make solo decisions?

• Are you highly self-motivated and persistent?

• Are you a "risk-taker"? How would you feel if your home were used to provide collateral for loans?

• Does your family support your decision?

• Can you cope with the insecurity of an uncertain and irregular income?

• Are you confident in your ability to sell your ideas, products, or services?

• Can you control your finances? Could you chase and pursue any debts to ensure sound cash flow?

How to minimize the risk

• Research your market thoroughly: What demand is there for what you have to offer?

• Prepare a comprehensive business plan so you have a sound overall view of your scheme.

• Be realistic about investment and returns. Use the most cautious estimates of income or profit.

• Seek expert advice from accountants, bank managers, small business advisers, and lawyers.

• Borrow as little as possible. Interest will be lower and risks smaller. If you want to expand, do it gradually.

• Consider whether it might be worthwhile to take a retraining course or learning an extra skill.

• Contact government agencies, which may offer career advice, retraining schemes, or financial support for courses. Banks are often a source of business start-up packages, which provide both funds and advisers.

Clarify your direction

Once you have as much information as possible, focus on two areas and investigate them further.

Take another close look at your own skills, experience, and qualifications. You probably have many talents you never had the opportunity to use at work, some of which might be highly relevant to your new career.

If you have the time, find out if you can work as a volunteer or part-time in any organization of special interest to you. This can be a source of invaluable experience—and contacts.

You probably already have a network of friends, acquaintances, and former colleagues; ask them whether they know anything about your proposed new position or career, or whether they have useful contacts. Try to find people who are actually working in similar positions or organizations.

Once you have launched yourself on a new career, you may doubt the wisdom of your decision. Give yourself time to adjust to what is a great upheaval. Periodically reassess your situation—try to be honest about how you feel and what you want—and adapt your methods or goals accordingly.

On your own

Starting your own business may hold great appeal. It offers freedom, flexibility, control, and potentially good earnings. There are problems, however, that you should seriously consider:

• An irregular or uncertain income

• Long hours

• No company "perks"—holidays, sick pay, medical plan, or pension plan

• Social isolation.

Bear in mind that your bank manager or financial partners may be more demanding than an employer. You may also have to develop skills in many new areas, such as sales, management, and financial control.

Changing direction may be the bravest thing you ever do, but it may also be the most rewarding, giving you the chance to direct your energies to what you really want and use your skills to the full.

RETIREMENT

ALTHOUGH MOST PEOPLE look forward to retirement, fantasizing about all the freedom they will have, it can actually be a time of loss: of unfulfilled professional dreams and of an important part of your identity, too. Retirement can trigger a crisis that is not just about ageing, but about changes in status, self-esteem, earning power, and aspirations. For those who have never fulfilled all their ambitions, this period can be extremely difficult. This is why it is essential to think long and hard about your goals throughout your life, and to understand the things in life that are important to you.

Although you may need time to come to terms with the end of the working part of your life, you can plan for this great change—and for the best ways to fulfill yourself during your later years.

Your many roles
The real you is made up of many different "selves," including your home self, family self, your secret self, and your work self. During certain periods of your life, you have to concentrate on one part of your life: If you are raising young children, for example, you know you need to spend more time with them, so your family self dominates over your secret self. But someone who has depended on work as a source of strength and identity will suffer more from retirement than someone who has a variety of interests outside work.

For example, workaholic Alan was completely preoccupied with his career, and for 25 years his job had also provided all his social, emotional, and financial support. When he retired, he had no social network or interests. He gradually lost energy, became depressed, and eventually became ill.

Sarah, on the other hand, always had interests outside her teaching job. Although she loved her work, on retirement she was able to become more involved in her amateur theatre group, started a youth section, and was able to spend more time with her family and friends. Although she missed work, she found new energy and enthusiasm for her leisure pursuits, made new friends, and was able to enjoy her retirement.

Changing gears
Shifting work patterns are changing the whole concept of work and retirement. Also, the line dividing home and office is becoming blurred, a social change that has many repercussions. If you are self-employed, it may be possible to go on

RETIRING GRACEFULLY

The best thing you can do is plan ahead while you're still working. Once retired, you will have much more free time, and you may find the lack of structure disconcerting, but you can use the opportunity to make your life more rewarding, interesting, and full.
• Make the effort to develop interests and hobbies outside work, even if you think you don't have time.
• Try to make friendships outside work, and get to know your neighbors.
• Get involved in your community. Consider whether you could help with school or municipal activities.
• Start adult education classes, on your own or with a friend or partner, and study something completely new—perhaps a language, a craft, a new skill, or a course leading to a qualification.

• Travel whenever you can, going to places you have never seen; now you have the time to explore your own area and country more thoroughly, too.
• Go out with groups as well as on your own or with your partner. The group could be composed of a circle of friends you already know, or you could join a new group and meet an entirely new set of people.
• Keep fit and look after your health, as well as your appearance. Find an activity you really enjoy to help keep you motivated, or join an exercise or dance class to make keeping in good shape a sociable activity. Taking care of yourself will help you enjoy life, keep you agile and supple, and benefit your self-esteem.
• Make the effort to stay active, interested, and curious—there's a world out there to discover.

Your many different selves
Our personalities have many components, and we can usually express only part of who we are in any one situation. Retirement may offer the chance to devote yourself wholeheartedly to your favorite activities, and to express yourself more fully.

working in some way beyond the usual retirement age. If you are ending employment with a company, it might be possible to negotiate a gradual reduction in hours. You can continue to give the company the benefit of your long experience while loosening the ties with the office set-up, thereby easing into retirement. This gradual adjustment is preferable to the sudden shock of finding yourself with little to do.

Whenever you decide to retire, your newfound freedom offers a wonderful opportunity to do everything you never had time for: learning new things, acquiring new skills, spending time with your family and friends, building new friendships, or simply reading and relaxing.

If you think positively and plan ahead, retirement could be a time of enormous freedom and rejuvenation—truly the "time of your life."

IN THE MONEY

SUDDENLY COMING into a vast sum of money must surely be one of the most common fantasies. The idea of winning a fortune on the lottery, say, or of being left a handsome legacy, conjures up pleasant dreams of spending the rest of your life on an endless holiday, wearing expensive clothes, living in a fabulous house, and never having to work again. It is an alluring dream, but perhaps dreaming about it is the wisest thing to do. The sudden acquisition of wealth, unlike a gradual improvement in your standard of living, can bring a number of problems in its wake.

Can you buy happiness?

It is easy to imagine that sudden wealth would automatically guarantee long-term happiness, but this seems not to be the case. Research in many countries has examined the outcome for people who have won large sums. One U.S. study of 22 lottery winners found that they were actually no happier than non-winners. Another study of 191 British winners revealed that, although they were slightly happier than average, they also had to contend with serious problems.

An interesting finding of the U.S. study was that winners found it hard to take pleasure in small things. While most of us enjoy many simple activities—watching TV, going for a country walk, eating with friends—winners of very large sums find their enjoyment diminished: Winning brings such a "high" that everything afterward seems flat.

The drawbacks

People who become rich through winning may find that everything changes too quickly. They may feel euphoric, but also bewildered and out of control. In addition, they may have to contend with:

• Envy from friends and family, as well as from neighbors and acquaintances.

• Requests for "loans" from family and friends, who don't expect to pay the money back, and begging letters from complete strangers.

INHERITED WEALTH

A more common way of coming into money is through an inheritance after a relative or friend has died. How you feel about this will depend largely on the relationship you had with the deceased. If you inherit an heirloom or artefact, this may prompt positive memories of the person who has died, which can be cathartic, although you may also be reminded of your grief and loss. If the deceased was someone close, you may find you have very mixed feelings about your newfound wealth, including any or all of the following:

• **Guilt.** You feel bad because you have the money only because your loved one has died. You may feel that if only you could give it back, you would be able to bring the person back to life somehow.

• **Lack of ownership.** You may feel it's not really "yours" because you didn't earn it; it's the fruit of someone else's hard labors, so you feel that you can't spend it or enjoy it.

• **Tension.** Legacies can trigger conflict, envy, and resentment within families, particularly if there are unresolved tensions about favoritism. The bereaved people's feelings of loss, anger, and pain may be misdirected into arguments.

• **Pleasure.** You know it was the person's wish for you to have the money and that he or she would have been pleased to know that you are enjoying it and spending it wisely. It is a link with the person you have lost, providing a sense of continuity.

You may find that you finally arrive at this last stage only after going through the more difficult and painful phases of grief. Realizing that the person you loved was thinking of you and wanted to leave you something is ultimately comforting.

A surprise windfall
Coming into money suddenly can change your life for the better, but it can also overwhelm you with the burden of unexpected problems. Take your time and seek professional advice.

• Doubt and insecurity that people—even old and trusted friends—may only be pretending to like them because of their money.

• A sense of anti-climax when the realization sinks in that, although money can improve a person's material circumstances and lifestyle, it cannot solve all their problems. People may still get ill, worry about their children, or argue with their partner.

• Feeling displaced if they move to a larger house and a different area. People may feel between two camps—no longer fitting in with their old neighbors, nor yet at ease with their new ones. If they have moved to a more expensive area, they may worry that their new neighbors look down on them.

• Confusion about identity if they have always worked, and then suddenly give it up. Even if they disliked or had lost interest in their job, people often miss the daily contact with colleagues. Some also feel useless and purposeless without the structure and sense of identity that work can provide.

The cautious approach
If you come into a large sum of money, it is vital to keep your head. Try to stay calm and rational.

• Do not give up work immediately. Think carefully about investing in any new work you might want to undertake.

• If you *must* have a wild spree or throw a big party, fine: Set up a separate account for this purpose.

• Sound financial advice is essential. Consult a recommended, independent financial adviser—preferably not a relative—who can help you invest wisely. Put some of the money in a no-risk savings plan.

• Taking a holiday is not only a treat: Away from the pressures and demands of others, you can consider carefully the kinds of changes you want to make.

• If you want to alter your lifestyle radically, plan how you could do this in stages rather than trying to do it all at once. Try to ascertain which features of your current life it would be important to retain.

CHAPTER FOUR

HEADING FOR A CRISIS?

CAN YOU RECOGNIZE when you might be heading for a crisis? Or are you frequently taken completely by surprise, only to realize that there were warning signs you overlooked? This chapter explores how different people react when a crisis is looming, and how you can spot trouble on the horizon—and be better prepared.

Many of us have periods in our lives when we feel overstressed because there are too many changes going on at once—for example, planning a wedding and moving house. Are you in danger of "crisis burnout"? If so, you may be heading for disaster. Use our stress-assessment scale to determine whether you are on the brink of an upsetting change (see "Crisis Overload?" pp. 80-81).

All crises, whether major or minor, are periods of transition, and no crisis, no matter how bad it is, lasts for ever. The changing situation may ultimately have a positive outcome, or at least a satisfactory resolution, but it may be a bumpy ride along the way. "Stages of Crisis," pages 82-83, defines the different phases of a crisis, and goes on to describe how people try out various responses and work toward resolution. Other articles will help you deal with a sudden crisis (pp. 84-85) or a long-term crisis (pp. 86-87).

Although we all suffer periods of stress at some point in our lives, we don't all react the same way, and some people are more susceptible to stress-related illnesses, such as heart disease. You can find out whether your personality puts you at greater risk of succumbing to stress, and how you might modify traits that undermine your health and well-being by turning to "Personality and Stress," pages 90-91.

"The Body Under Pressure," pages 92-93, explores the mental and emotional stress that might affect you physically. Sometimes, physical symptoms, such as migraines, tension in your neck and shoulders, and skin disorders, can be the way you express inner turmoil or feelings that you find it hard to talk about.

"Danger! Stress Rising!" on pages 98-99 will alert you to signs that indicate you may not be coping well. Remember, however, that some degree of tension can be stimulating. The questionnaire "Good or Bad Stress?" on pages 96-97 will help you find out if your current stress is productive or destructive. You may discover that a difficult situation is actually helpful: forcing you out of a rut, making you take risks in unexpected directions, and bringing out your best—perhaps previously undiscovered—talents and strengths.

ANY CRISIS THREATENS YOUR STABILITY AND SECURITY, BUT YOU CAN LEARN TO RECOGNIZE AND RESPOND TO WARNING SIGNS. BY BEING MORE PREPARED, YOU CAN MINIMIZE THE IMPACT OF POTENTIAL PROBLEMS.

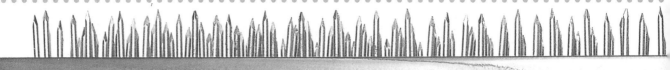

There is no magic formula for a stress-free life. You can aim to keep stress at a minimum by having a low-stress job, leading a healthy lifestyle, and making sure that you set enough time aside for relaxation; what you cannot do, however, is avoid bereavement, domestic crises, or a number of other events that are simply a part of life. How stressed are you? Do you feel you are going through a rough patch, with one crisis after another? If so, your stress level could be dangerously high. More worryingly, if you have had several stressful events in succession, it can certainly affect your health and your ability to relax. In addition, if you become accustomed to the feeling of living "on the edge," and are used to having at least one crisis on your hands, you may not realize just how much you need a break—or how great a toll the stress may be taking on you. Use the stress-assessment scale on the right to determine whether your stress level is too high and if changes need to be made.

Adapting to change

All change, including positive change, is stressful because we have to adjust mentally, physically, and emotionally, and the loss of what is familiar tends to make us feel insecure in some ways. The more momentous and painful an event is, the more we must make an effort to cope with it.

It is also true, however, that the degree of stress we suffer is dependent on our attitudes and expectations. For example, one person might react to becoming unemployed with bitterness and feelings of being a failure, while another might see it as an opportunity to change direction and build a new life based on what he or she really wants.

During the 1960s, doctors Thomas Holmes and Richard Rahe examined the hospital records of 5,000 patients, and discovered that significant life events—both good and bad—had occurred in the months preceding the patients' illnesses. From this research, they developed a scale that measures the degree of stress associated with these events.

Check your stress level

Using the adaptation of the Holmes and Rahe life-events scale shown here, tick the number of difficult or important events that you have experienced in the last two years. Then grade each event you ticked on a sliding scale from 1 to 10, with 1 indicating that the event hardly affected you, and 10 that it affected you a great deal. Add up all your number ratings to arrive at a final total, then read the conclusions in the far-right column.

Life events

1. Death of a spouse or partner
2. Divorce or end of a relationship
3. Separation from a loved one
4. Imprisonment
5. Death of a close family member
6. Serious injury or illness
7. Getting married
8. Unemployment or being dismissed
9. Relationship problems (or reconciliation)
10. Retirement
11. Illness of a close family member
12. Pregnancy
13. Sexual problems
14. Birth of a new baby
15. Change in your financial situation
16. Death of a close friend
17. Change in the nature of your work
18. Start of a new relationship
19. Arguing more—or less—often with your partner

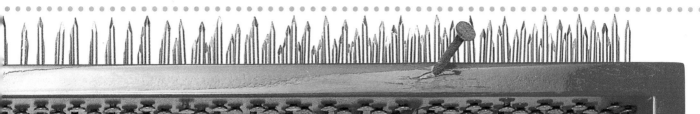

20. Increased/new bank loan or mortgage
21. Financial difficulties
22. New responsibilities at work
23. A child starting school
24. A son or daughter leaving home
25. Problems with relatives or close friends
26. Disputes with neighbors
27. Achieving an important personal goal
28. Partner starting or stopping work
29. Starting or leaving school or college
30. Change in living conditions (e.g., taking care of an ailing parent in your home)
31. Change in sleeping habits
32. Problems with employer or colleagues
33. Change in working hours or conditions
34. Moving house
35. Changing school/place of study
36. Taking up a new sport or hobby
37. Change in religious or spiritual life (e.g., going to church more frequently or less often, or losing or gaining faith)
38. Change in your social life
39. Serious legal problems
40. Change in the frequency of family get-togethers
41. Change in your eating habits (e.g., starting a diet, cutting out particular foods)
42. Going on holiday
43. Having family members visit
44. Minor trouble with the law (e.g., parking offences)

How did you score?
• **1–30:** Indicates that the last two years of your life have been remarkably stress-free.
• **31–55:** Low to moderate level of stress.
• **56–80:** Medium to high level of stress
• **81 or more**: Indicates a very high level of stress; you need to reduce your stress load.

The higher your score, the greater the possibility of stress overload, which might make you more vulnerable to illness and disease, depression, and even mental breakdown.

Reducing stress
If your score is high (81 or more)—and especially if you have felt stressed for a long time—it is a good idea for you to have a break and get away from it all. As well as helping you wind down and relax, it allows you to take a fresh look at your life, and to consider ways in which you might reduce or be less adversely affected by any stress in your life. Don't choose a complicated trip that demands a great deal of planning.

If you have experienced several major stressful events within the last two years, it is probably wise not to introduce any additional change into your life, such as moving house or changing your job, unless it is unavoidable or if sticking with the status quo will cause you even greater stress.

Finally, consider whether you can learn anything from your score: Are there events you could have foreseen or prepared for? This might help you avoid destructive behavior patterns and contribute to better stress-management techniques. Several articles in this book will help, such as "Learn to Relax," pages 120-121, and "Releasing Tension," pages 122-123. If things look bleak, turn to "Asking for Help," pages 132-133.

Life at the sharp end
Having too many stressful events can overwhelm you, making you feel that life is always fraught and laden with hazards, with no hope of respite.

STAGES OF CRISIS

ALL OF US SEEK TO CREATE order and predictability in our lives, which is why it's easy to be thrown off balance when something out of the ordinary or an unexpected change occurs. Remember that a crisis is a transitional period that offers a chance to improve your coping strategies, thereby enhancing your sense of self-esteem and self-worth. Although an unfamiliar event has the potential to become a full-blown emergency, you might effectively contain or diminish its negative effects if you think of it as a process with distinctive stages. Viewing it in this way also makes it less daunting: It is easier to accept the difficult phases you may have to work through on the way to resolution.

HOW GREAT IS THE RISK?

At any stage, the level of perceived risk may go up or down, but you will be better able to cope with a situation if you can gauge what level of risk it poses.
Level 1: Voluntary and predictable
This kind of situation is the least threatening. You believe you understand the challenges, have the skills to influence events, and can predict the outcome. For example, pursuing a career as a teacher involves choosing to have training, deciding how to specialize, and perhaps improving your communication skills.

Stage 1: Disruption

Comfortable habits can be disrupted by a problem or a threat to carefully laid plans. The first response of many people is "tried-and-true" behavior—previously successful strategies that have been learned. For example, if you have a new manager at work, you would probably act in the same way as with your former manager—but this might not be appropriate. Or, if you have been feeling tired, you might think it's because you have been working late and simply need to have a few early nights.

What to remember
• Try to discover what may be unusual about the situation you are currently facing.
• Try to ascertain which factors could be seen as stimulating and enjoyable rather than threatening.

Stage 2: Trial and error

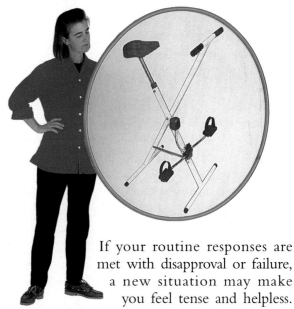

If your routine responses are met with disapproval or failure, a new situation may make you feel tense and helpless. You may try other strategies in an attempt to restore the equilibrium of a known pattern. For example, your new manager may have objected to your chatting about topics unrelated to work, so you approach him or her only to discuss work in a serious manner. If you do not feel renewed after light exercise and rest, you might try to exercise more and to eat more healthily.

What to remember
• Try to recall previously learned skills to help restore your confidence and diminish tension.
• Try to be flexible; if you ask for advice, take note of what others say, but make your own decision.

Level 2: Voluntary and unpredictable
Some events or situations are voluntary but unpredictable: You may anticipate a likely occurrence but cannot always determine the outcome, a position firefighters or police officers often find themselves in. Getting married is also a good example of this: You make the decision to commit yourself to a partner, and may make your best efforts to maintain a good relationship, but unforeseen changes in personality, behavior, or circumstances may affect the marriage.

Level 3: Involuntary and unpredictable
This type of situation poses the greatest risk to your coping skills, self-esteem, and sometimes even your life. Being assaulted or coping with the sudden onset of a debilitating illness are examples. Certain strategies can limit unpredictability; for example, you can install security systems to reduce the risk of burglary, and not smoke to reduce the risk of lung cancer. By trying to anticipate how things might go wrong, you can protect yourself from a full-blown crisis.

Stage 3: Make or break

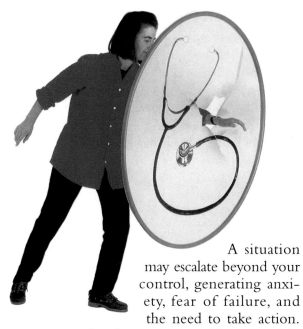

A situation may escalate beyond your control, generating anxiety, fear of failure, and the need to take action. If your manager has been unreasonable, you might apply for other jobs or confront him or her. If you think your fatigue is the sign of a serious illness, you might ask your doctor for a frank diagnosis.

What to remember
• Ask yourself if it is the best time to resolve the situation. Choose a time when you feel strong, and try not to provoke a negative outcome.
• Ask yourself if the problem could be coped with if you changed your goals, expectations, or aspirations. Redefine the situation and motives.
• Focus on the most important factors.

Stage 4: Breakdown or breakthrough

At this stage, you may feel demoralized and unable to cope. This is truly the "crisis" phase of an event, yet even if you don't achieve the outcome you want, there may be other benefits. You might learn greater flexibility in your professional behavior by dealing with a difficult manager. In coping with an illness, you might find stamina and courage.

What to remember
• Focus on goals that are still attainable.
• Generate new goals that are more appropriate.
• Feel free to ask others for help and support.

SUDDEN CRISIS

The most terrifying type of crisis is the unexpected one, the event you cannot see looming over the horizon, but which suddenly appears in front of you. Finding yourself against your will in the middle of an unpredictable event is perceived to be the most threatening thing in life (see "How Great is the Risk?" pp. 82-83). Experts in crisis management believe that some of the observable responses to trauma are more extreme or prolonged when a crisis overtakes you "out of the blue." These responses seem to correspond to the following stages.

Stage 1: Denial or outcry

You create order and predictability in your life based on what you consider most important. In a sudden crisis, however, this type of selective attention is severely challenged. For example, after a car accident, people seem to deny the event because they cannot recognize the strangeness of the situation: They say things like they "couldn't believe" what was happening. Sometimes, even in the face of a crumpled vehicle, the same phrase is repeated as they struggle to comprehend exactly what has occurred and what the possible ramifications will be. It is a normal response to be "dazed" by an overwhelming reality, and in this phase most people are incapable of any action or activity.

Others, however, are stirred to action immediately. Compelled by the need to restore "justice," they actively seek to discover the cause of the crisis, a reaction described as "outcry" behavior. An outcry response frequently generates overactivity, vehemence, and "blaming." People may run around in circles, desperately seeking to restore their previous situation.

Occasionally, victims of a sudden crisis find it difficult to move beyond a cycle of denial or outcry, or—depending on the severity of the crisis—find that it takes them a very long time to accept what has happened. If they are unable to discuss their feelings—if, for example, there is no-one to listen to them when they say things like, "It was so frightening, it was like a blow to my chest, I just couldn't move"—victims of a sudden crisis may develop physical symptoms of severe stress, such as blinding headaches, an inability to eat, trembling, heart palpitations, and panic attacks. The sooner help and psychological support is available from friends and family or trained counselors, the sooner these symptoms subside, enabling the person to come to terms with what has occurred. Should symptoms persist, however, post-traumatic stress disorder may develop (see pp. 60-61).

What to remember
- Depending on the nature of the crisis, people may be unpredictable, or act in ways that are "out of character." For example, people who were previously independent and pragmatic may appear "shaky" and unable to cope.
- When a crisis occurs suddenly and "out of the blue," this stage is frequently the longest.

Stage 2: Reality "sinks in"

A significant finding of crisis management research is the discovery that most people are strongly motivated to respond to a crisis—that is, they rarely try to evade what has happened, even if they think they can't cope.

During this second stage, moments of panic and exhaustion are interspersed with moments of insight. Along with unwelcome flashbacks, there may also be deliberate efforts to recall the precise nature of what has occurred. For example, if you were badly injured in an automobile accident, you would probably talk about the accident with your family and friends, trying to remember relevant details. You would also talk to your doctor about how long you would be expected to stay in hospital, and what long-term effects there might be. You might want to contact the police, too, about the cause of the accident and any other vehicles involved.

What to remember
- Deliberate recollection is an important way to gather the strength needed to deal with what has happened.
- The "unbelievable" aspect of a sudden crisis slowly begins to fade.

Stage 3: Starting over

Most of us prefer to think long and hard before making any changes, but with a sudden crisis, we can deliberate only *after* the event, not before.

What to remember
- Any crisis is a decisive turning point and a journey into unknown territory. Never feel ashamed to ask for advice, and don't be reluctant to accept offers of help.
- Above all, trust in your ability to find your way through suffering, and to draw your own map toward recovery. The more you believe in your strength, the more resilient you will be.

Out of control?
Probably the most frightening thing about a sudden crisis is that you may feel completely powerless to control what is happening.

LONG-TERM CRISIS

Many crises come to a definite conclusion so that you can begin to rebuild your life, despite the fact that you may be left with lingering feelings of regret or disappointment. There are other types of crisis, however, that cannot be resolved easily or quickly, situations that remain difficult to cope with for many years and for which a solution appears beyond your reach. Crises of this type demand not only a great deal of physical and emotional stamina, but qualities such as patience, determination, and flexibility. You may also need more support from other people.

THE LONG HAUL

Unlike a short-term crisis, it is difficult to determine when—or even if—resolution of a long-term crisis is possible. Try to view your situation as an open-ended process, and strive to develop these helpful characteristics:

• **Be realistic.** While you must never give up hope, you must acknowledge the seriousness of whatever problem you face.

Chronic illness or recuperation
A chronic physical condition—diabetes, heart disease, or certain types of cancer—may require that you modify your diet or take medication.
What to remember
• If you must change your diet, become a creative cook. Many specialist cookbooks are tailor-made to make living with a chronic condition easier. Continue to take pleasure in food and the social ritual of sharing meals with friends and family.
• Try not to resent the tedium a disciplined drug regimen imposes. Instead, view it positively as a way of maximizing your health and energy. Discuss side-effects with your doctor so that you have the most appropriate medication and dosage.

Divorce
A bitter and protracted divorce can be exhausting and demoralizing.
What to remember
• Recognize that creating a new family situation takes time and effort. Concentrate on creating a new "team" with shared goals and aspirations.
• Take advantage of your newfound freedom. Spend time only with supportive friends (both old and new), and doing things that you enjoy.
• Don't waste time being bitter or full of regrets. Try to learn what you can from the experience about your needs and expectations, explore new interests and set new goals—and move on.

• **Be flexible in your approach to problem-solving**. Consider different coping strategies, such as trying alternative therapies as an adjunct to traditional medicine to treat a serious illness.

• **Pace yourself**. In a short-term crisis, people usually feel compelled to marshal all their energies at once so that they can focus on the resolution. During a long-term crisis, however, resolution may be clear one minute, vague the next, or not apparent at all. Pacing yourself will help you to see your situation as a long journey, during which you walk steadily forward rather than force a conclusion.

• **Conserve your strength**. Whatever situation you face, try to maintain your own well-being. It will then be easier to sustain the belief that life still has a great deal to offer.

The job you hate

An environment where everyone is unhappy is a mixed blessing: Like-minded colleagues can be supportive, but you may also feel depressed by a negative atmosphere. Even worse is to be the only one who is unhappy. What can you do if you must continue working, or cannot change your job?

What to remember

• No matter how demoralized you feel, try to do your best work. You will then have the satisfaction of doing a job well, even if you get little thanks or recognition from your employer.

• Try not to identify who you are with what you *do*. The more you can establish interests and hobbies outside of work, the happier you will be.

An unhappy marriage

You may be unhappily married, but feel that you cannot leave your partner for a variety of reasons.

What to remember

• If you stay together for the sake of your children, demonstrate to them that you respect your partner, even if you do not love him or her.

• A partner who is an invalid or incapacitated in some way may be the reason you stay. Ask for support in order to maintain your sense of identity (see "When to Take a Break," p. 47).

• For some people, the fear of financial insecurity and loneliness may be reason enough to stay married. In this case, try to rebuild your relationship so that neither of you is harmed by staying together.

FIGHT OR FLIGHT?

WHEN YOU ARE confronted by a problem, when you are tense or in a dangerous situation, you respond physically, even if you are unaware of it. This is known as the "fight-or-flight" response, and is intimately linked to the part of your brain that controls instinctive survival responses. It triggers changes in your body that influence whether you stand your ground and confront the threat head on—in animals, this occurs not just when they growl or hiss, but also when they "freeze" to make themselves invisible to a predator—or flee for safety. Frequently, there is no time at all between the perception of danger and the response: Animals suddenly bolt and seek cover, and people have an inbuilt "startle" response.

Changes in the body

The physiological changes in the body are carefully orchestrated, immediate responses.

• The adrenal glands, which are located on top of the kidneys, secrete two hormones, epinephrine and norepinephrine. These substances play an essential role in the fight-or-flight response, stimulating physiological changes that you may be aware of but do not consciously control.

• The heart beats more rapidly and strongly. This increases the blood flow to the muscles so that, if danger persists, you can run away (the "flight" response). Alternatively, you have more muscle power to overcome the threat (the "fight" response).

• Breathing deepens as tiny tubes in the lungs, called bronchioles, become wider to take in more air. As a result, blood pumped by the heart to the muscles is rich in oxygen.

• The liver helps to raise levels of blood glucose, a type of sugar, which provides the energy needed to fuel muscle power. You may feel restless or "jumpy."

• The pupils become larger, enabling you to take in more visual information about your immediate environment so you can see any danger more clearly.

• Hairs on your head and body may stand on end because small muscles are stimulated to contract. In animals, this makes them appear larger (and so more fearsome).

• The sweat glands are stimulated. Sweat pores, especially those in your armpits and hands and on your forehead, open, and you begin to perspire. This helps to cool the muscles that, because they are working hard, are heating up rapidly.

• All the body systems not needed to defend against a threat, such as digestion and urination, slow down in order to provide more blood and thus more energy to your muscles.

SEE WHERE YOU ARE

Throughout the day there are constant, involuntary changes to the size of your pupils. Sensory receptors in your eyes respond to light and to the proximity or distance of objects. In addition to this, during moments of heightened awareness—that is, when you're evaluating a situation that is interesting or frightening, or when you're attracted to someone—the muscle fibers surrounding the pupils are stimulated by nerves to contract: The pupil then widens to let in more light.

Anxiety can work for you

Competitors in some sports, notably track and field events, are sometimes encouraged to imagine themselves in a terrifying situation—to imagine, for example, that they are literally running as though their lives depended on winning. Their imagined fear stimulates the fight-or-flight response, and the corresponding surge of energy is thought to improve their performance. Although you may never have to run for your life, there are still situations where the instinctive fight-or-flight response can work for you. Remember that it is meant to protect you, making you more alert so that it is easier to respond to a rapidly changing or threatening environment.

Although few of us think we need to cultivate our instinctive responses, there are still situations that are threatening, and our instincts can be a reliable way to determine the degree of danger so that we can cope well. Instincts help you decide when a situation is potentially dangerous or threatening, and also help you to remain vigilant. Knowing about your own instinctive responses will also help you recognize when someone else is afraid or anxious, or when they feel nervous, "jumpy," or threatened. They may perspire or tremble, or their breathing may become more rapid. In order to defuse a potentially awkward or dangerous situation, you may decide, for example, to "back away" during a tough negotiation in a meeting, or steel yourself to remain calm and immobile when confronted by someone who is threatening you with a weapon.

Take a deep breath

If you find yourself in a situation that is not life-threatening but you're breathing quickly, your pulse is racing, and your palms are sweating, you're probably about to perform a task that risks failure or a critical loss of your self-esteem. Perhaps you're waiting to take an important exam or dive off a high board. Whatever the level of risk or danger, you have perceived the situation as a point of no return, or the turning point of a crisis. Your best strategy is to do what athletes are trained to do: Visualize a successful outcome, take a deep breath, and—when you feel ready—do your best.

Confront or flee?
Your body may react to a stressful situation in the same way our ancestors reacted to a predator or other threat, but you can modify your fight-or-flight response through visualization or stress-management techniques.

By becoming aware of the size of other people's pupils and noticing which situations tend to trigger this change, you can sometimes tell a great deal about their mood, because they cannot control this response. Fear is not the only feeling revealed by enlarged pupils: Sexual interest is also signaled in the same way. Certain therapeutic drugs (such as those used by an ophthalmologist during an eye examination) as well as some "hard" drugs also affect pupil size.

PERSONALITY AND STRESS

IF YOU WERE STUCK in a traffic jam, would you be likely to rev your engine, toot your horn, and make three telephone calls on your mobile phone? Or would you switch off your engine and just patiently sit and read or daydream?

In 1974, two American cardiologists suggested that a person's susceptibility to heart disease could be predicted by their general temperament and typical response to stress. Two categories were proposed, Type A and Type B. Type A people tend to be hyperactive, impatient, and are therefore highly stressed. Type B people, on the other hand, are less driven and more adaptable, tend to be more aware of themselves, and can control their stress levels more effectively. Most of us are a combination of the two. In the box below are typical characteristics of Type A and Type B people. The more Type A qualities you recognize, the more prone you may be to stress-related illnesses, including heart disease.

The Type A person

If you are predominantly a Type A, you may not even bother to read these two pages, but will only scan the lists below and move on. Despite an apparently extroverted nature—frequently associated with an aggressive competitiveness—a Type A person is typically more inhibited, anxious, and lacking in confidence in social situations than a Type B person, although this may not be obvious.

The compulsive need to be in control and to achieve goals quickly stems from a deep sense of inadequacy. As children, Type As may have felt that they could never do enough to please parents who had high expectations but little patience. Type As frequently feel they will only be loved for their achievements, never for themselves, and are prone to stress-related illnesses. Frequently, it is only when they become seriously ill that they recognize their harmful behavior and learn to slow down.

WHICH TYPE ARE YOU?

Knowing your typical characteristics will help you control your levels of stress more effectively, thereby achieving mental equilibrium.

Type A people:	Type B people:
Find it hard to wait	Can wait patiently
Tend to be very competitive	Relate harmoniously with most people
Feel over-responsible for everything	Feel only limited responsibility
Are always in a hurry	Are rarely in a hurry
Are preoccupied with work and have few hobbies	Have a wide range of interests
Need attention and recognition from others	Try to satisfy and fulfill themselves
Are careful about details	Are not very precise
Can't leave things unfinished	Can leave things incomplete
Constantly strive at work but feel unfulfilled	Feel satisfied with work done
Interrupt others or finish their sentences	Are good listeners
Are hard-driving	Are easy-going
Do everything quickly	Do things slowly
Are often impulsively angry	Are rarely angry
Speak quickly and forcefully	Speak slowly and calmly
Keep their feelings inside	Express their feelings easily
Often set unrealistic deadlines	Set appropriate deadlines

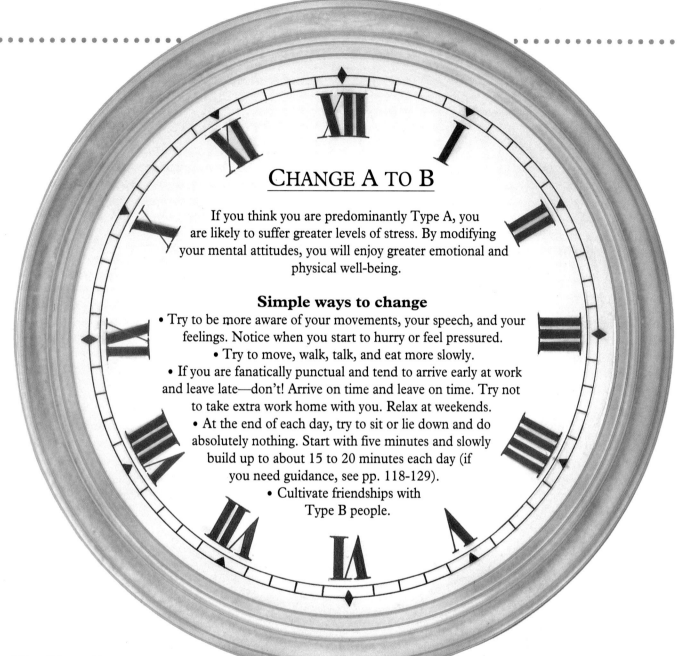

CHANGE A TO B

If you think you are predominantly Type A, you are likely to suffer greater levels of stress. By modifying your mental attitudes, you will enjoy greater emotional and physical well-being.

Simple ways to change

• Try to be more aware of your movements, your speech, and your feelings. Notice when you start to hurry or feel pressured.
• Try to move, walk, talk, and eat more slowly.
• If you are fanatically punctual and tend to arrive early at work and leave late—don't! Arrive on time and leave on time. Try not to take extra work home with you. Relax at weekends.
• At the end of each day, try to sit or lie down and do absolutely nothing. Start with five minutes and slowly build up to about 15 to 20 minutes each day (if you need guidance, see pp. 118-129).
• Cultivate friendships with Type B people.

The Type B person

If you're a Type B person, you're more likely to be introspective, and to reflect on your own behavior and that of others. Type Bs usually have a much more relaxed, benign view of themselves and the world than Type As. They are able to accept and enjoy themselves because they have thought about their own inner values, and are less susceptible to the opinions of other people. Self-respect is very important to them. They don't need to be fiercely competitive with others, or to prove themselves. Although typically they are much more secure and gregarious than Type A people, they may sometimes find it difficult to be assertive, or to be clear about the strategies required for achieving their goals.

Type B people are more likely to have felt loved by their parents for who they were, not for what they did. Because they feel less pressure to achieve and compete, they feel greater contentment.

Are you a combination?

Most people are a combination of both types. For example, you may be a Type B when you feel relaxed and secure, but behave like a Type A under stress. By knowing what situations trigger Type A behavior, you can learn to act like a Type B person by staying calm, being patient, and doing things slowly.

THE BODY UNDER PRESSURE

Our bodies don't always know the difference between stress, pressure, and danger. Whether you're watching an exciting film, facing an exam, or your car just missed hitting another one, your body will react in the same way: Your heart will beat faster, your breathing will increase, you may break out in a cold sweat, or feel "butterflies" in your stomach. Once the event has passed, however, your body will slowly return from this state of heightened arousal to normal. Your body reacts in a similar way whether the danger is "real" or "imagined," which is why both mental and emotional stress affect you physically.

The slippery slope of stress

Whether you're climbing a treacherous mountain or having to deal with a sudden crisis, your body will shift into a "survival mode" of heightened arousal. If you are continually feeling stress, your body will remain locked into this "fight-or-flight" mode. Some people feel like this almost all the time, while others experience it only once or twice in a lifetime. Even if stress lasts for a few days or weeks, or if you are not aware of stress, it can have a profound effect on your physical health. Imagine how it affects your body if you are stressed for months or even years.

Mind and body

Stress does more than simply increase your heart and pulse rate. Each of us has a unique way of responding to stress, which may produce a specific set of symptoms. Perhaps you have a "weak stomach" or a skin disorder that flares up when you're under pressure. Conditions that commonly appear or worsen when we are under stress include:

• Headaches, including migraines
• Tension or stiffness in the neck and shoulders, and in the lower back
• Skin disorders, such as eczema
• Colds and flu
• Asthma
• Stomach and bowel problems
• Heart palpitations.

Some of the above symptoms are congenital, meaning that you were born with a weakness in that part of your body. Others develop as a way of expressing something, almost like a metaphor. For example, nausea is associated with disgust, a pounding heart with fear, a "pain in the neck" with anger; similarly, skin disorders tend to be highly visible and so may be a way of telling the world you need help.

The effect of stress
Too much pressure not only undermines your health, but may contribute to feelings of exhaustion that leave you less able to cope.

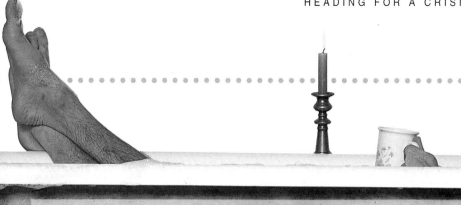

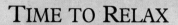

TIME TO RELAX

If you find yourself in a stressful situation, or are anticipating one, there are ways you can minimize pressure and maintain your health. Try the following suggestions:
• Take a long, deep bath, scented with a relaxing bath gel or an aromatherapy oil.
• Gentle exercise, such as a walk or a swim, may help clear your mind.
• Let yourself daydream or use guided imagery (see pp. 128-129).
• Work with your hands. If you have a job that involves a great deal of thinking or mental stress, a craft or hobby such as sewing or model-making can be relaxing.

You can discover which part of your body tends to react to stress by keeping a diary for a month or two. Whenever you don't feel well physically, write down a brief description of your symptom as well as what is happening in your life at the time. You may notice that a pattern starts to emerge; for example, you might have a tendency to get colds when you're tired or a headache when you're under a lot of pressure at work. Knowing what triggers a symptom may help you modify your behavior, or respond sooner so that you can effectively manage the level of stress. You might, for example, go to bed an hour earlier to get extra rest when you know you risk becoming run down, or make sure you have a relaxation session as part of your day (see "Learn to Relax," pp. 120-121).

Long-term stress
If the stress is combined with exhaustion or fatigue, your body will be less able to cope, and more vulnerable to infection and disease. In the short term, this may not be very serious; in the long term, however, a minor symptom could become a debilitating illness. People subjected to long periods of stress or exhaustion frequently become ill; this may start with flu, or a cold from which you never quite recover, and lead on to more serious illness or repeated bouts of exhaustion.

Physical signs
There seems to be no question that the state of your mind and feelings can have a profound effect on your health. So-called psychosomatic illness (see "All in the Mind?" pp. 94-95) has often been dismissed, partly because of the difficulty in drawing a clear line between something that is "imagined" and something that is "real." In some ways, this is a false distinction—pain is always real, whether its source is physical or emotional.

A physical reaction to stress may be a way of expressing feelings that can't be let out in another way. You may think your feelings are frightening, unacceptable, or uncontrollable, or that you have to be "strong" and that showing emotion is "weak." For example, Karen, who was under immense pressure at work, started to develop severe migraine headaches, which forced her to take time off. Ted was unable to grieve after the death of his mother and suppressed his feelings; several months later, his doctor found that Ted had developed heart disease.

You may recall that there have been times in your life when emotional distress had a physical manifestation in this way, but by learning how to express your feelings, and taking time to relax, you will safeguard your well-being.

ALL IN THE MIND?

WITHOUT CONSCIOUSLY realizing it, you are always responding to the signals your body is sending. You probably recognize when you're tired because you start to yawn, but this action occurs as an automatic response to the fact that your depleted muscles need more oxygen. You may then become aware of the fact that you are doing things more slowly or your concentration has diminished, so you take a break and rest. What you might find surprising is that just as your body reacts to changing physical needs, it also responds to your thoughts and feelings. Anxiety or internal conflict may thus undermine your health.

Denying feelings

All of us are capable of defending ourselves against unpleasant thoughts—sweeping our feelings under the carpet—because these feelings are too painful or frightening to face. Sometimes this strategy, known as denial, is necessary and appropriate, such as when you must put aside your own fear to administer first aid to an injured child.

If this coping strategy is overused, however, there is a danger that the feelings will be pushed so far away that you are no longer aware of them at all. But the feelings still exist and may find physical expression, either in the form of an illness or chronic problem, such as stomach problems, or as tension, which you may try to relieve by biting your nails, grinding your teeth, or clenching your fists.

Dissociative disorders

When people are very anxious or disturbed, symptoms may not be physical but psychological. A type of disorder may then occur in which an aspect of the personality—a certain memory, set of characteristics, or behavior—is separated (or "dissociated") from normal consciousness or a person's sense of identity.

The most common example is amnesia, a loss of memory that has no physical cause, such as a blow to the head or alcohol or drug abuse. What is forgotten may be a traumatic or painful incident, but the memory may return in the future, perhaps as a recurring nightmare or an obsessive thought that often appears to be completely unrelated to a person's current life situation. Amnesia often occurs after a particularly frightening incident (see "Post-Traumatic Stress," pp. 60-61), and it may last for hours, weeks, or years. Psychotherapy is usually recommended.

Anxiety and the body

It's easy to understand how stress can contribute to a migraine headache or to high blood pressure, especially if a person is overtired, eating the wrong foods, and working too hard. Visible or obvious physical symptoms caused by an outlook or an emotion are known as *psychogenic*. Both the symptom and the attitude can be treated.

There are, however, more serious types of disorder where the mind/body connection is less obvious. For example, some people express their anxiety not by talking about their problems but by becoming preoccupied with minor physical symptoms, such as a cough, which they are sure are signs of a more serious illness. In these cases, there is a symptom but the cause is exaggerated.

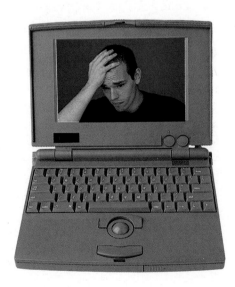

TELL-TALE SIGNS

Physical symptoms that are not obvious to others and for which there is no detectable bodily cause may be the result of a conversion disorder. This type of illness, called *psychosomatic*, may occur when a person feels unable to ask for help. Symptoms often provide clues to the unconscious psychological problem. They "show" that help is needed, and may be one of the following three types:

• **Sensory.** Pain or loss of sensation or function is common; blindness not caused by infectious disease or an injury is one example. The symptoms may be created because a person is too traumatized to "see" the reality of a painful situation.

• **Motor.** A deeply buried psychological trauma may result in an inability to perform certain actions, causing disorders such as paralysis or an inability to speak, or to swallow or breathe normally.

• **Visceral.** Severely anxious people sometimes display a wide range of medical conditions, including pregnancy, even though sexual intercourse or fertilization has never taken place.

When there are no apparent physical causes of an illness, a doctor will usually then look for one or more of the three tell-tale signs of a psychosomatic disorder:

• **Inconsistency.** Symptoms may come and go quite suddenly or dramatically (genuine symptoms usually take longer to appear or resolve). The feelings a person describes and the appearance of the symptoms may also be contradictory.

• **Selectivity.** The symptom or dysfunction, such as paralysis or a headache, may only appear in specific circumstances or in the presence of certain people.

• **Indifference.** Although a person may discuss a symptom at great length, a doctor may nonetheless sense that he or she seems strangely detached from the threat of a serious illness: It does not seem quite "real" to him or her.

Conversion disorders

Another type of disturbance in the mind/body connection is conversion disorder, which is characterized by a major change—or even a complete loss—of normal physical activity, although there are no medical findings to explain why something has gone wrong. The disorder, which is rare, is so named because a source of stress is "converted" into a physical problem, which usually does not last long. During the Second World War, for example, several bomber pilots developed night blindness and thus could not carry out their nighttime bombing missions. Because the military doctors who examined the pilots were unable to find any damage to their eyes or to the optic nerves, they concluded that the young men were suffering from conversion disorder, which reflected their fear and anxiety about the danger they faced.

The different types of conversion disorder are described more fully in the box at the top of the page. It is important to realize that these disorders serve the purpose of temporary relief from stressful situations and are cries for help; for this reason, psychotherapy is usually helpful.

GOOD OR BAD STRESS?

We tend to think of all stress as bad, but there is a tremendous difference between the stress of overwork that can wear you down and make you tense and moody, and the excitement of working hard at your personal pet project, or the exhilaration of doing some exercise that you enjoy. Actors know that without some degree of stage fright their performance would lack an edge or sparkle. Similarly, if you don't feel any anxiety before making a speech or delivering a presentation, you probably won't perform as well.

The type of stress that excites you, gets you moving, and adds zest to your life is "good," or productive, stress, while that which wears you out or limits your creativity and drive is "bad," or destructive, stress. This exercise will help you determine the types of stress in your life. Tick the comments that apply to you, then read the conclusions on page 140.

At work

1. I feel able to deal with most problems in a cool and efficient way.
2. I can look at problems objectively and fairly.
3. I remain calm under pressure.
4. I can leave my work behind at the end of the day so I can enjoy my evening.
5. I find my work challenging and satisfying.
6. I enjoy working with a team of people.
7. If there's something I need to discuss, I am able to do this right away.
8. I can express my anger or dissatisfaction reasonably and appropriately.
9. I can be assertive when necessary.
10. I often feel I have to work in the evenings and at weekends.

11. I am often on edge and irritable.
12. I've had more than one argument with a colleague or my boss.
13. I feel chronically weighed down with too much work and not enough time.
14. I often feel I'm being treated unfairly.
15. I find it difficult to say no when someone asks me to do something.
16. I am often bored and frustrated.
17. I tend to take long lunch breaks, and look for any excuse to get out of work.
18. I always look at the job advertisements.

Relationships

1. I have close friends whom I see regularly.
2. There's someone in my life to whom I can talk openly and honestly.
3. I like to meet new people.
4. I generally feel at ease with people, and can enjoy myself and relax.
5. If I feel angry or annoyed with someone, I'm able to tell them so.
6. If I want to be alone, I can say so.
7. I enjoy being part of a group.
8. I enjoy being with people, even if they're not particularly "my type."
9. I don't have many close friends.
10. If I feel down or angry, I tend to withdraw until the mood has passed.
11. I often feel used by people.
12. If I'm angry with someone, I keep it to myself.
13. I rarely invite others out with me.
14. I tend not to open up to people, even those to whom I'm closest.
15. I don't like groups, or doing things with others.
16. I'm nervous with people I don't know.

Physical health

1. I generally feel in good health—alert, energetic, and in good spirits.

2. Although I have the odd ache or pain, I tend to get on with life.

3. I haven't been ill for over six months.

4. I tend not to "catch" colds or flu.

5. I don't smoke, and I don't overeat or drink alcohol more than I should.

6. I take good care of my health but am not particularly obsessive or fanatical.

7. I regularly play a sport that I enjoy or take part in an exercise or dance class.

8. I feel young for my age, but can accept the fact that I will grow older.

9. I sleep well and have a good appetite.

10. I feel full of aches and pains.

11. I have one or more of the following: stomach/bowel trouble, skin disorders, headaches, palpitations, joint pain, backache.

12. I worry about becoming seriously ill.

13. I read a lot of books about health and illness, and then worry about myself.

14. I tend to feel run down and completely exhausted by the end of the week.

15. I don't sleep well, have trouble falling asleep, or sometimes wake early.

16. I take either stimulating or tranquilizing drugs.

17. I'm overweight, eat junk food regularly, smoke, and/or drink too much.

18. I am worried about growing old and worry excessively about my appearance.

19. I'm always on a diet but can't seem to lose weight.

20. I'm anorexic and/or bulimic.

21. I find it difficult to enjoy life because of physical pains or illness.

Creativity

1. I have a hobby or craft that I really enjoy and regularly spend time on.

2. I often think of new and different solutions to problems.

3. I don't always do things "by the book."

4. I like to travel and do new things.

5. I'm interested in other people, how they think, and what makes them tick.

6. I enjoy painting, writing, music, or some other art—doing it or appreciating it.

7. I like to discuss and explore ideas.

8. I have a wide variety of friends and acquaintances from different walks of life.

9. I voice my opinion, even when it's different from what others think.

10. I find it easy to imagine things.

11. I've never tried a new hobby or considered taking a course in something new.

12. I tend to leave being creative to others; I've never thought of myself as creative.

13. I don't like change, and usually avoid it if at all possible.

14. If someone suggests doing something on the spur of the moment, I usually decline.

15. I find it difficult to let go and completely be myself or express myself.

16. I'm not sure about art and I don't tend to say what I like in case I'm "wrong."

Productive or destructive?

Good stress can help you be productive and creative; bad stress can make you feel your life is unraveling and that you're falling apart.

DANGER! STRESS RISING!

YOUR MIND AND BODY can cope with an enormous amount of stress, but there comes a point when rising stress levels can threaten your mental or physical well-being. Some people have to reach a point of intense physical or emotional pain before they recognize they need help, but when all is not well, there are usually early warning signs, such as:

• Sudden anger
• Mood swings
• Chronic fatigue
• Carelessness or clumsiness
• Neglecting your appearance
• Feelings of depression.

Even if you are skilled in covering up your worries—so much so that you often hide them from yourself as well as others—you should not ignore these warning signs, for they indicate that the demands of your life are exceeding your capacity to cope, and you should take immediate action to reduce the stress in your life (see pp. 118-129). These first steps will break the vicious circle, and will help you to see your situation more clearly, and to find ways to act more effectively.

Rising temperature

If these early warning signs are ignored or not acted upon, things can often get worse. To ward off increasing stress, or to stifle feelings of despair or loss of self-esteem, people may turn to alcohol, drugs, or food as a source of comfort. However, relying on these unstable props for support is a dangerous strategy, one that is short-lived and likely to generate new problems.

Those who abuse alcohol may drink alone, go on binges, or not remember being drunk, all of which seriously affects their work and relationships. An addiction to drugs will often be denied by the addict, who, meanwhile, is getting into financial difficulties paying for his or her habit. Eating disorders such as anorexia nervosa or bulimia may be difficult to detect, but an obsession with body image, addiction to exercise, and delusions about food and eating are obvious indicators. The anguish these compulsions cause is traumatic for those who suffer from them, and for those who try to help, who may see only too clearly that the mental health of someone they care about is at risk.

HELPING SOMEONE ELSE

People whose behavior is self-destructive may feel ashamed and fear discovery, and so problems may remain undetected or unacknowledged for a long time. Such deception may only exacerbate the problem and further damages their precarious self-esteem. What can you do to help?

• Approach them with an expression of concern for their general well-being, and offer to listen to their problems. It may open a door so that difficulties can be faced constructively.
• Talking about your *own* problems sometimes encourages people to talk about theirs, thereby helping them to realize they may have a problem.
• Persevere: The more serious a problem is, the more likely it is to be denied—and your offers of help rejected. A gentle, persistent interest will build trust, as will persuasion that professional help might be of benefit. Having the names of support groups at hand is a good way to provide support—offer them with encouragement.

Extreme stress can also affect the mind, causing irrational or erratic thinking, confusion, or phobias, such as a fear of heights or of public places or of the dark—or sometimes of a person who previously had been trusted. Obsessive thinking—mulling over the same things again and again, so that a person can think of nothing else, and focusing on one thing or person to the exclusion of all else—can be a sign of mental disturbance. In very extreme cases, people may hear voices telling them what they should think or feel, or become paranoid, feeling that everyone is against them or that they are being controlled by others.

Mood swings, especially from a depressed state to one of manic hyperactivity, can lead to uncharacteristic behavior, such as spending too much money, which frequently leads to serious debt, or being unrealistic about work and taking on too many commitments—behavior that risks failure.

No relief?

Problems that come at you from all directions will cause stress levels to rise, and you may feel there is no escape.

Don't hide—ask for help

Very occasionally, the disappointments of life can precipitate feelings that life is not worth living. A situation can seem so unbearable that anything seems better than carrying on. If you feel like this, take action right away. You may have been brought up to feel that you have to be strong and self-sufficient, so that asking for help can take a great deal of courage, but it is vital that you do. Perhaps you can talk to a friend; if additional support is needed, your doctor can help you find the most appropriate way to recover or re-establish your equilibrium: There are many different types of support group or therapy. Remember that seeking help is the first step on the road to recovery.

CHAPTER FIVE

LIVING THROUGH CRISIS

WHILE FEW PEOPLE would actively seek to create a crisis, many usually learn a great deal by coping with a challenge—no matter how difficult it may seem at the time. This chapter focuses on your ability to evaluate or avoid a crisis, how you react—as well as the origins of your response—and how to keep yourself going, or to get the help you need when a situation threatens to overwhelm you.

Do you tend to overreact? Or are you flexible enough to respond appropriately whatever the situation? "Assessing a Crisis," pages 102-103, includes a questionnaire to enable you to check if your responses are appropriate. It also offers a five-step strategy to help you cope.

All of us react differently to a crisis, and how you respond depends to a large degree on your upbringing and what you learned from your family. Perhaps you were the sensible, efficient one at home who could always be relied upon to sort things out; if so, you may find it hard to turn to others for help when you need it (see "Overcoping," pp. 108-109). Understanding the roots of your behavior, and your strengths and weaknesses, will help you act in a more considered and effective way in the future (see "Know Yourself," pp. 110-111).

If you tend to take on other people's problems, you may be in danger of over-burdening yourself and succumbing to stress. You may also make it harder for another person to take responsibility for his or her life. It is important to know how to set appropriate boundaries: when to help and when to say no. In this way, you can avoid being either overinvolved or unsupportive (see "Someone Else's Crisis," pp. 114-115, and "Whose Crisis Is It?" pp. 116-117).

A crisis that creates great stress may also take its toll on your body. Eating good, nutritious food, exercising, and learning how to relax will all help to keep your energy levels high, thereby improving your ability to cope (see "Listen to Your Body," pp. 118-119, and "Learn to Relax," pp. 120-121).

Can you ask for help when you need it or do you try to struggle on alone? "Finding Support," pages 134-135, will help you discover where to turn. "Hope in Crisis," pages 136-137, describes how even the worst crisis may bring you closer to those around you. At the very least, a crisis allows you to discover what your strengths are. With these insights, you will be better equipped to face—and to prevail over—any future challenge.

FOCUSING YOUR ENERGY AND CONCENTRATION ON FINDING

A WAY PAST THE OBSTACLES WILL BRING YOUR CRISIS TO

A SUCCESSFUL RESOLUTION.

Assessing a Crisis

ARE YOU THE SORT of person who makes a mountain out of a molehill? Can you recognize a mountain when you see one? Or are you so detached that you can't see a crisis coming until it's too late to take action? Learning to assess a crisis and evaluate its real importance will help you react appropriately and act sensibly.

If you're feeling particularly low or stressed, problems that you would normally take in your stride can seem overwhelming. Imagine that your children have been impossible all day. They have quarrelled, tormented the cat, and dragged muddy feet across the carpet. Then you find that the washing machine has leaked all over the kitchen floor; in your fraught state, this "last straw" turns into a "major" crisis. The suddenness of a crisis often causes panic and confusion, but you can learn to control and modify your responses, many of which you may have unconsciously picked up from your family. You will be most effective, and make more sensible decisions, if you can keep a sense of proportion and a cool head.

Clear thinking is the key to problem-solving, so once a crisis has arisen, try to remember that it is usually unwise to make a hasty decison in the heat

Can you keep a cool head?
Even if you tend to act impulsively, you can still learn how to stay cool in a crisis and plan an effective strategy.

Do You Overreact?

Do you know how you habitually respond in a crisis? Try this quiz, choosing **a**, **b**, or **c**, according to how you'd be most likely to react.

For conclusions and analysis, turn to page 140.

1. *Your teenage daughter is home an hour late from a night out with her best friend. Do you:*
a) Consider the most likely reasons for their lateness, such as missing the bus, and decide at what time you will contact other parents or the police? When she gets home, discuss her lateness with her?
b) Feel very anxious, and call the friend's mother to find out if the girls are there?
c) Panic and imagine the worst, and call the hospitals, the police, and the friend's mother every five minutes? When your daughter gets in, shout at her, then cry with relief?

of the moment. If you feel panicky or pressured by other people, try some deep breathing exercises (see pp. 120-121) to help you wind down and reduce your anxiety so that you attain a calmer frame of mind. You may feel better if you give vent to your feelings, perhaps by talking your situation over with a friend, relative, or your partner.

Once you have calmed down, you will be ready to take effective, appropriate action. Tell yourself you can cope, and you will. Just remember this simple five-step strategy:

• **Stop.** Never act in haste. Even if the situation is urgent, or if people are badgering you, remember that you will always make a better decision if you take time to think things through. Consider the worst possible scenario. Often, you realize that even the worst that can happen is not the end of the world. If it is really dire, at least you have now faced up to it, which will help you deal with it.

• **Think.** Consider your options for action. It may help to discuss them with someone else, or to write them down, to clarify them in your own mind, or to view the problem from several angles.
• **Plan.** Anticipate the practical details of your solution, and consider how to put them into practice. Be realistic about what is possible.
• **Act.** Carry out your plan, consulting with anyone else affected by your actions.
• **Evaluate.** Check the results of your actions at intervals. If other factors come into play, be ready to be flexible and change your strategy—or even to revise the outcome you thought you wanted.

People who have coped with very serious crises often say they have learned valuable lessons, the most important of which is that they learned to keep things in perspective. All the minor irritations of life—the car breaking down, or the cat breaking your favorite vase—assume much less importance.

2. *You suddenly realize that you have left your papers for a very important meeting in a taxi. Do you:*
a) Explain what has happened, but carry on with the meeting and do your best without the notes?

b) Try to keep a low profile at the meeting while feeling tense and panicky, and dreading that someone will ask you a question?
c) Rush out of the building without telling anyone what happened, then telephone to say you are suddenly terribly ill and can't attend the meeting?

3. *A friend you are sharing a meal with suddenly gets a piece of food stuck in his throat and starts to choke. Do you:*
a) Calmly use your first-aid skills to remove the obstruction quickly, then reassure your friend afterward?
b) Slap him on the back, and shout for help, not really knowing what is best?
c) Faint at the sight of his distress, coming around when the crisis is over?

4. *There's a power cut, your computer malfunctions, and you lose a day's work. Do you:*
a) Consult the manual or computer services about what can be done to regain your work, then make notes of what you can remember?

b) Complain that you've lost all your most important files and wait until someone else sorts it out?
c) Get upset about your lost work and refuse to accept help, having decided that the situation is hopeless?

5. *You have planned an important dinner party, but, at the last moment, you accidentally drop the main course on the floor. Do you:*
a) Throw it away, confess to your guests, and rustle up something else with gusto and humor?
b) Serve it up anyway, but spend all evening worrying that someone will notice?
c) Burst into tears, say it's all hopeless, and let someone else take control?

STEERING CLEAR OF A CRISIS

Not all crises are inevitable. In fact, many can be avoided by sighting potential dangers on the horizon before they have a chance to become unwieldy or even dangerous, thus undermining the stability of your relationships or work life. A simple example is that of small children in the kitchen, who can be a serious hazard to themselves and others. By storing knives, crockery, and glassware in unreachable drawers and cupboards, never leaving pan handles to overhang the stove to be bumped or grabbed, and instilling discipline about the inherent dangers from an early age, many potential accidents and crises can be avoided. Similarly, a pregnant woman can avoid a crisis by being prepared for a possible premature delivery. She can keep an overnight bag packed, and always carry the telephone numbers of her doctor, partner, and perhaps a babysitter for her other children.

Mapping out a plan
It is not only practical crises that can be avoided by a little careful thought or forward planning. Emotional upheaval can also be minimized by understanding how unsettling certain events might be, and by mapping out a strategy that will lessen their impact. For example, when children go to school for the first time, their mother can prevent a crisis for them by talking about what happens in school, describing the activities and the new friends they will have, and by showing them the school before the first day so that it is not completely unfamiliar or frightening.

Getting the crew on board
When Peter and his wife, Betty, asked his 78-year-old widowed father to live with them after he had had a bad fall, Peter recognized the potential practical and emotional problems, especially the fact that their 13-year-old daughter, Susie, would have to give up her room to share with her 10-year-old sister, Louise.

In the weeks before his father's arrival, Peter got the whole family together to discuss the various concerns each of them had.

Spotlight the crisis
By recognizing and focusing on potential hazards, you can plan and take appropriate action to avoid the worst problems.

For Susie, it was the prospect of losing her privacy that upset her most. But because the bedrooms had high ceilings, Peter thought they could build Susie a large sleeping deck with curtains, which she could draw across the entrance. He suggested that the raised structure could have a shelf for her books, and a small music system with headphones so Susie could listen to music in private. Although Susie would no longer have her own room, she felt her father's proposal sounded fun and was a compromise she could live with.

Betty had a demanding job and was concerned about the extra work required to look after her father-in-law, especially because he would only eat very plain food while the family enjoyed more exotic fare. Peter agreed to take on more of the family cooking, and the weekly menu was varied to accommodate everyone's tastes.

Peter recognized that when a new person comes to stay in any family home, adjustments must be made by everyone. By discussing each area of potential dispute and planning for the event, disruption was kept to a minimum and family harmony was maintained.

Can you spot the rocks?

Any major event—even positive ones such as going on holiday or getting married—can precipitate a crisis because the unexpected may occur.

You should try to make sure you've checked and prepared for as many eventualities as possible. If you were planning a boat trip, for example, you would listen to a weather report, make sure you had lifejackets on board, and ensure your boat was "shipshape." You wouldn't dream of setting out to sea when a storm was looming. By anticipating a crisis, you have the opportunity to take control so that your situation does not turn into a full-blown drama.

THINK WHAT YOU WANT

Question: When is a crisis not a crisis?
Answer: When you don't think it is.

How you view a situation very often determines how you will respond, and maintaining a sense of proportion about an event that threatens to be overwhelming will help you cope. Try to be realistic about the relative importance of a particular problem within the context of your life as a whole. Positive thinking and other mental strategies such as "reframing" (see "Check Your Beliefs," pp. 130-131) are methods that can be effective and help you to achieve a better perspective.

Think again

Janet's son, for example, announced he was giving up his law studies to become an actor. She saw it as nothing but a tragedy: As far as she was concerned, he was throwing away his future—as well as her ambitions for him.

In her fatalistic scenario, he ended up as a struggling actor, unable to earn a decent living, with no other skills to fall back on. Her son felt that she had no sense of proportion about his seriously considered decision. Although dismayed at her lack of faith in him, he nonetheless proceeded to study drama, and had no contact with his mother for an entire year.

Janet finally realized that her stubborn attitude meant that she would "lose" her son. In effect, she "reframed" the situation, accepting that while the life of an actor is unpredictable, it was better for him to give up a career he felt would be unfulfilling and lead to unhappiness in later life. She decided to put her faith in his talent and judgment, gave him her support, and was thus able to share in his joys and sorrows. Her reframing exercise enabled them to build a more rewarding relationship.

How We Learn to Cope

OW YOU RESPOND to a crisis is influenced by many factors, but perhaps the most important is the memory of how your family coped with change. Even if life experiences have modified your early or distorted impressions, or you rebelled against your family's habitual way of coping, few people manage to leave family influences behind completely.

Were you overprotected?

In some families, children never get the chance to find their own feet because they are gathered up into someone's arms the moment they falter or stumble. Although overprotective parents may think they have their child's best interests at heart by rushing to help, they may be undermining his or her confidence and autonomy. The parents may have hidden reasons for their behavior: they may be fearful themselves, never having developed professional or social interests, or they may be jealous or possessive of their children. Whatever the reason, overprotected youngsters may become powerless adults. If you were raised to believe that the only safe place in the world was within the bosom of the family —and that the world outside the home was threatening and dangerous—it may be difficult to cope with or surmount unexpected changes in circumstances. Events that could be seen as a challenge, such as taking on new responsibilities at work, may be seen as very intimidating.

If, during your childhood and adolescence, you were given advice that warned you about life's disappointments, rather than stimulating you to consider life's possibilities, you may still feel less than confident about making independent judgments or taking a

Did you feel safe?
Family members should feel safe both within and outside the family home, not made to feel that the world outside is fraught with danger.

IS THE PAST PRESENT?

Overwhelming feelings are a natural response to a traumatic event, but do spend some time, perhaps with a friend, trying to decipher whether your feelings and expectations are unduly influenced by the past. Ask yourself the following questions about your current crisis. You might feel more comfortable writing your answers down:

• Can you describe the event, your feelings, and your expectations of the crisis?

• Who are the people you think will help you, or judge you harshly? Why?

• Can you ask for help?

• Have you felt this way before? If so, when and why?

If you recall a similar past event, ask yourself the same questions about the previous situation: who helped you, what you thought would happen, what actually occurred. Are there any key people involved in your current crisis that remind you of someone in the past? Do you feel trapped in the earlier situation?

You might find, for example, that an employer who has fired you with no warning reminds you of an envious older sibling who bullied you. Instead of resorting to a heated confrontation, you could remain calm, remind yourself that you are a responsible adult and not a powerless child, and make an appointment with the personnel manager to discuss your legal rights.

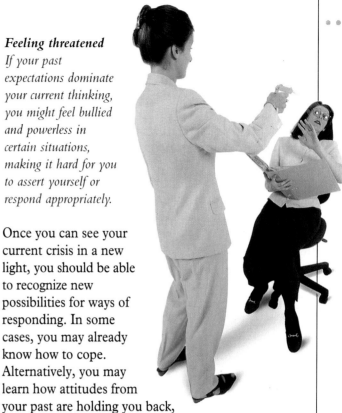

Feeling threatened
If your past expectations dominate your current thinking, you might feel bullied and powerless in certain situations, making it hard for you to assert yourself or respond appropriately.

Once you can see your current crisis in a new light, you should be able to recognize new possibilities for ways of responding. In some cases, you may already know how to cope. Alternatively, you may learn how attitudes from your past are holding you back, or making your current situation worse. If you can release yourself from a rigid way of thinking or feeling, you will have greater choice, and can be more hopeful about a positive outcome.

---

calculated risk. If you were made to feel helpless, or that someone else would solve your problems, you may find even minor tasks, such as telephoning a plumber, daunting. How can you change?

• Realize that it is never too late to assert yourself. This may be hard to do if you feel you have no right to resist offers of "help."

• Begin to take responsibility for certain key areas of your life. Start with small tasks; with each success, your confidence will undoubtedly increase.

Was your family unsafe?

Unlike overprotective families, which at least try to establish the family home as a place of refuge, some dysfunctional families are not only unhappy but threatening. In such environments, people may feel unsafe because they are bullied or humiliated when they become angry, upset, or sad. In some families, feelings may be expressed in inappropriate, frightening, or violent ways, leading to physical or emotional abuse. Family members learn to stifle, rather than express, their feelings, and there is little attempt to discuss or understand feelings or behavior. If someone has been profoundly hurt or disappointed, he or she may despair of ever being heard or helped, and this pessimism may be the basis of later expectations in life. Such people often continue to think, "No-one is going to listen to me, so I'll just have to deal with this myself."

Children from unsafe families like this may become adults who find it very difficult to risk self-exposure. They are emotionally inhibited and find intimacy threatening. During a crisis, they typically feel ashamed and afraid of punishment—and are often acutely lonely.

All of these feelings and learned behavior, however, can be remedied, especially if children or adults have the opportunity to meet other families—through friends or partners—who express feelings honestly and solve problems effectively.

OVERCOPING

There are some people who seem to be at their best during a crisis. Immensely capable, they continue to cope efficiently with the practical details of life—making sure that the house still remains tidy, seeing that everyone is fed and ferried to work and school, and dealing effectively with people and paperwork. These enviable strengths, however, often hide the fact that they—like the people they appear to be helping—are afraid: of losing control, of reaching out to others for help, or of facing their real or unconscious fears. As such, they may be paying a very high price for playing the role of Superman or Superwoman.

What is kept hidden

Frantic coping behavior can be a way of denying a difficult situation or painful feelings. For example, when Rachel's mother became terminally ill, Rachel wanted her to be cared for at home, and was determined to become a very efficient nurse. She learned how to give a bed bath, changed the sheets every day, and studied nutrition thoroughly. She thus managed to care for her mother with very little help. Even though she had to work harder as her mother became increasingly frail, she would let no family members or close friends relieve her of what she saw as her "duties."

By concerning herself only with the day-to-day problems of her mother's care, Rachel was avoiding the painful realization that her mother was going to die. By controlling the many details of the time the two of them had left to share, she could pretend to have some sway over the hand of fate.

Although Rachel might have asked for help, the function of her frenetic activity was to keep her fears at bay until she could begin to cope with her denied grief. In due time, she began to realize that her efforts could not save her mother, but provided the time she needed to prepare herself and to gain the strength to face her mother's inevitable death.

Controlling others

Rachel's caregiving activity demonstrated a protective defense mechanism known as displacement, which occurs when ideas or feelings are shifted from a threatening situation, and are expressed or acted out in a different way until the truth can be faced.

Less helpfully, however, overcoping behavior can be relentless and inflexible so that an individual's vulnerable, fearful, or anxious side is never revealed. Moreover, "overcopers" or "rescuers" who are out of touch with their own feelings can be insensitive to the feelings of other people affected by a crisis. Overcopers may become

---

FIND PEACE FOR YOURSELF

Use the following questions to prompt self-analysis and identify any tendency to be an "overcoper":

• What do you feel and think while you perform your caregiving tasks? Do you feel guilty, resentful, or panicky, or that everything will collapse unless you—and only you—do something?
• How do you deal with unwelcome feelings?
• What would you feel if you stopped "rescuing" and let others help *you*? Or if you had free time?
• Do you use drugs or alcohol to cope with stress?
• Do you ever cry or get angry about certain aspects of your life? Do you try to repress these feelings?
• Are you answering these questions honestly?

You don't have to be a tower of strength all the time. If you feel isolated and under strain, do not hesitate to seek help from a trusted friend or perhaps a counselor. Don't be afraid to lean on someone else for a change.

Weary of your role?
If you feel isolated or under strain, it may be time to stop being everyone else's nurse and to look after yourself.

A shield of "strength"
People who cope well during a crisis may be sincerely compassionate and protective of others who need their help. Sometimes, however, they may be shielding their own vulnerability, loneliness, and fears.

dictators who impose their own, "right" solutions. For example, Rachel's older brother felt that he had to make all the funeral arrangements. Although he thought he was helping Rachel, he neglected to ask her what she thought their mother would have preferred. Rachel felt excluded, disregarded, and distressed, especially because she had been the one who, while caring for their mother, had discovered that she wanted a large, festive, non-religious memorial service instead of a small, private family funeral.

Although denial and displacement mechanisms get people through the most painful part of a crisis, opting for overcoping activities—and trying to control other people—in order to distance yourself from the turmoil of your inner life may ultimately backfire, resulting in more desperate attempts to numb unacknowledged pain. Some people turn to alcohol or drugs, substances that can cast a rosier glow over harsh reality. For example, Rachel's brother, whose need to organize was a way of feeling in control, started to drink too much because he felt guilty that he was unable to care for his mother the way Rachel had. When he had come to terms with his mother's death, he stopped drinking.

Were you an over-responsible child?

The role of Superman or Superwoman is often adopted by those who are accustomed to sorting out other people's problems from an early age.

Most children can sense when adults in the family are unhappy or unable to cope. A child may act as a nurse or a social worker for an ailing or alcoholic parent in order to keep the family together, and also to get love and recognition.

Many children who assumed responsibilities at too young an age carry the painful memory of their often futile attempts to make things better well into adulthood. They continue to be "rescuers" because it is the only role they have known, or because it is the only role that makes them feel they have value and are worthy of love. Frequently, such people are very lonely because their overcoping behavior makes other people feel useless, controlled, or not needed, and, without knowing it, they undermine the chance for genuine intimacy with other people. Sadly, many rescuers feel they have no right to ask for help when *they* need it—even from close friends or partners—because they cannot express their own past fears and sorrows.

KNOW YOURSELF

MOST OF US LIKE TO THINK that we know ourselves but, because most crises are unpredictable (see "How Great is the Risk?" pp. 82-83), we can never be entirely sure how we will react. It helps, therefore, to become familiar with your own strengths and weaknesses so that you can harness your best qualities and attributes to deal with problems in a calmer and more balanced way.

Harness your strength
During a crisis, you may discover that you are stronger and more capable than you think you are.

Reach in or reach out?

When reacting to a crisis, do you become intro-spective, turning inward and relying on your own resources? Or do you reach out toward others? Do you do this because you trust that they will want to help you, or because you fear being responsible for what may be a bad decision?

Consider how one couple, Marie and Tony, responded to a crisis: When they decided to divorce, Marie telephoned her sister and close friends, who all encouraged her to share her feelings of hurt, anger, and disappointment.

Tony coped in a very different way, bottling up his feelings and spending more and more time alone. After a few months, he realized that he needed to talk to a counselor, who would not be involved in his life in any other way.

Although Marie's and Tony's different responses—one extroverted, the other introverted—reflected their different temperaments, both eventually recovered from the pain of separation.

Thinking or feeling?

Your personality will largely dictate how you cope in a crisis, and one significant way people differ is that the responses of certain people are based on thinking, while others respond more emotionally. If your approach is largely cerebral, you will:
• Identify what you think about a particular situa-tion, and tend to mistrust your gut feelings.
• Try to be objective (even when you are too involved for this to be possible).
• Consider strategies to overcome the problem, and remain fairly distanced from it.

LIVING THROUGH CRISIS / KNOW YOURSELF

NOBODY'S PERFECT, BUT...

People deal with problems in many ways, some of them more effective than others. Below are some of the *least* effective ways people try to deal with problems. These defense mechanisms frequently create further problems in their wake.

• **It's not my problem**. This response is a denial of responsibility, and is an attempt to scapegoat outside factors or someone else. Sometimes uncontrollable outside factors *do* precipitate a crisis, but if a problem is your fault, admit it. Don't look to blame yourself or someone else; focus instead on solving the problem. Even if you have not caused a crisis, you may still feel morally obliged or compelled to help resolve it.

• **If I don't think about it, it will go away.** This very common response covers many types of avoidance strategies, which range from fairly harmless ones, such as oversleeping because you can't face what you think will be a bad day, to drinking too much to avoid the problems in your marriage, or at work.

• **It's all my fault.** Some people with low self-esteem blame themselves as a way of remaining passive and staying enmeshed in the problem. Others feel responsible for things over which they have no real control, such as when one person in a marriage feels responsible for the alcoholic behavior of his or her partner, rather than letting the other person deal responsibly with the problem he or she has created.

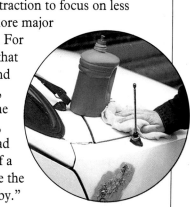

• **Look at less serious problems.** It can be a welcome, but unwise, distraction to focus on less serious problems when more major ones need your attention. For example, you may know that your car is falling apart and becoming unsafe to drive, but instead of checking the bodywork, motor, brakes, and tires, you focus instead on how the car looks, as if a new paint job will obscure the danger and you can "get by."

These responses are not wrong (everyone does them to some extent), but it's better to find ways to cope.

If, however, your reactions are predominantly emotional, you may tend to:
• Want to express your feelings and "trust your hunches" (your subjective responses).
• Be unaware that your feelings, especially if they are expressed vehemently, may sometimes cloud your judgment.
• Find it impossible to maintain a sense of proportion or detachment.

Trying to combine these two reactions can help: You should recognize your feelings and sometimes trust your intuition, but stepping back to evaluate your plan to cope will ensure a clearer overall view so that you can see a way out of the crisis.

Turning to others

During a crisis, one of the most difficult things to do is keep a sense of perspective, and you may find you need to turn to a reliable, honest friend to help you look at things in a clear light. Bear in mind, however, that the advice given by others is often colored by their own particular problems, experiences, and perhaps their expectations of you.

Sometimes, discussing matters with someone who is completely impartial such as your doctor or a counselor can help you see your own situation in a different way, making it easier to work out how you should proceed (see "Asking for Help," pp. 132-133 and "Finding Support," pp. 134-135).

HOW DO YOU REACT?

When confronted by a crisis, do you always respond in a predictable or even rigid way, or are you flexible, acting according to the situation and the people involved? Take a look at the scenarios below, and tick the answer that comes closest to how you would react in each situation. Add up the number of "a"s, "b"s, "c"s, and "d"s, and then turn to page 140 for conclusions and analysis.

1. *While out shopping in a department store, you hear a woman exclaim loudly that her purse has been stolen. She is obviously distraught and on the verge of tears. Do you:*
a) Approach her and offer your help, suggesting that she sit down with you so that she can talk through her experience and calm down?
b) Feel sympathetic but unsure about what to do, and find a member of staff to help, who you think will have the training to deal with this kind of problem?
c) Ask her if she saw the thief, offer to contact the police, and say she should cancel her credit cards?
d) Pretend not to notice, feeling that there is little you can do, and hope someone else will help?

2. *Your neighbor is a woman to whom you have always been pleasant, and sometimes chatted with casually. One day, as you say hello, she bursts into tears and tells you that her husband has left her and she doesn't know what to do. Do you:*
a) Help her into the house, and listen as she pours her heart out, saying you'll help her in whatever way you can?
b) Comfort her as best you can, but try not to get too involved, advising her to call a relative or friend?
c) Tell her things don't have to be that bad, and offer to put her in touch with your lawyer?
d) Not know how to handle it because you are taken aback by her sudden tears, say how sorry you are, then hurry back to your own house?

3. *Your closest friend has been trying to have a child for a long time. Now, tests have revealed that she is unlikely ever to conceive. She is devastated, but her husband doesn't feel the same way and she feels it may create a rift between them. Do you:*
a) Encourage her to cry for as long as she wants, telling her you realize how awful she must feel, and offer to speak to her husband?
b) Pass her some tissues, and sit with her until she stops crying, encouraging her to focus on the future by discussing her plans with you?
c) Give her information about adoption, in-vitro fertilization, and other options, which you have collected, while at the same time reassuring her that many women lead rewarding, fulfilling lives without ever being mothers?
d) Feel slightly irritated and impatient by her histrionic response, and try to cheer her up by distracting her?

4. *When he gets home from school one day, your teenage son tells you that he has failed all his exams. He feels he will never be good at anything. Furthermore, he refuses point blank to return to school, and says he may as well go for the first job he can get. Do you:*
a) Cuddle him as if he were a baby and reassure him that everything will be fine?
b) Ask him what he thinks went wrong with his exams, and talk through the situation until he is calmer, then discuss the possibility of retaking some or all of the exams?
c) Ring up the school immediately, explain your son's position, and ask for an appointment to see the head teacher as soon as possible?
d) Tell your son that he had better learn from his mistakes, make up a study schedule, and start knuckling down immediately to some serious hard work to prepare to resit his exams?

5. *You have a pleasant, but not close, relationship with a colleague. One day you are alone at work, and he says he has cancer. He is frightened and doesn't know what to do. Do you:*
a) Put your arm around him and encourage him to express his feelings?
b) Feel panicked by his news, but try to ask him calm and sensible questions about what is wrong?
c) Rush to find a book showing that this kind of cancer can be helped, and reassure him that it will all be fine?
d) Listen to him, but feel very relieved when other people return to the room?

6. *Business is going badly and your boss warns you that you may be made redundant because you have been there less than a year. Do you:*
a) Become deeply upset, beg your boss to reconsider, moan to your colleagues, and call all your friends?
b) Become upset but take the news calmly, phoning your partner or a friend, but without discussing it in depth until you leave the office?
c) Get angry, and spend the day calling all your contacts about possible work and writing job application letters?
d) Work on in silence, hiding how upset you are, while your workmates discuss the company's future?

Self-analysis
Understanding how you react in different situations reflects your deeper feelings and helps you vary your response according to the context.

SOMEONE ELSE'S CRISIS

WHEN SOMEONE CLOSE to you suffers a crisis, it is only natural to want to help, although it can sometimes be difficult to know what to do for the best. Good friends provide a vital support system during a crisis, but it is important that you take care of your own needs, too.

Exactly how you react to someone else's crisis will depend on what relationship you have with that person, what has happened, and whether it has a direct impact on you. For example, when Mary's best friend Fay lost her baby, Mary was a tower of strength. She was warm and supportive whenever Fay spoke about the baby, and she helped look after Fay's other children so that Fay and her husband could grieve together. However, three months later, when Mary's husband Ralph was made redundant, she found it very hard to cope. Ralph was the main breadwinner, and although Mary had a job, she didn't earn enough to support the whole family. She felt angry with Ralph and with his boss, anxious about how they would manage, and exasperated with what she felt were his inadequate attempts to find other work. For his part, Ralph felt badly let down by Mary.

After seeking specialized career guidance, Ralph suggested they see a counselor. His self-esteem improved and so did the family's finances. Mary also realized that she had been badly upset and affected by the death of Fay's baby, and that supporting Fay had drained her emotionally so that she could scarcely cope with her own family crisis.

How can you help?

Any support you can offer, whether emotional or practical, will be a tremendous help to someone in the throes of a crisis, and will ultimately serve to strengthen your relationship. Realize, however, that you cannot "save" or "rescue" anyone from their difficulties. The best you can do is strive to be patient and compassionate, while accepting that someone else's life is not entirely in your hands.

HOW MIGHT YOU FEEL?

• **Helpless:** When someone you love is suffering, you will want to ease their pain. This is not always possible, however, and it can be very difficult to accept that things won't all come right at once.

• **Angry:** You may feel angry at the situation that is making someone you love upset, and want to take revenge on anyone you feel has caused it. Alternatively, you may be angry at the person because you feel he or she may be partly responsible for the problem.

• **Upset:** When the person you care for is in pain, it is very difficult not to feel anguish yourself.

• **Vulnerable:** When a crisis strikes your friend, you may feel exposed to what suddenly seems like a dangerous world, and feel anxious and tense.

• **Frustrated:** After providing help and emotional support for a while, you may expect the person to be on the road to recovery. If he or she shows no signs of this, you may start to feel exasperated. You may also discover that you feel exhausted, and no longer want to act like an emotional sponge absorbing someone's else's problems.

• **Hesitant:** You might be afraid to get involved, fearing that you might only make matters worse or that you will give the wrong advice.

• **Bored:** If you have been supportive for some time, you may feel you've had enough—especially if you think someone is coping inadequately—and you may ask yourself: "How much longer can I listen to this?"

Without an outlet for these feelings and emotions, you may find someone else's crisis becoming your own as your stress levels rise. If so, try talking things through with a counselor.

Transferred feelings
It is easy to get drawn into the crisis of someone close to you, but becoming too involved may not help either of you.

WHOSE CRISIS IS IT?

When those you love are finding life difficult, it can be hard to differentiate between their problems and your own. However, taking on the responsibility of sorting out someone else's problems will simply make your life more stressful: It can be a way of avoiding your own difficulties or dilemmas, and you also allow that person to remain passive.

Is it your responsibility?

If you feel yourself becoming too involved, you may have to back away from certain crises, and allow those who are more directly involved the opportunity to work through the problem themselves. This does not mean that you should be unsupportive or uncaring—only that you should know where and when to draw the line between being helpful and carrying someone else's burden. This is not always easy. For example, while you might be fairly clear about your own and your colleagues' responsibilities at work, you may find it hard to assess how involved you should become in your adult children's difficulties. To understand more about your own boundaries, answer the following questions, choosing the response **a**, **b**, or **c**, based on how you think you would be most likely to react; then check your score and read the conclusions on the right.

Questionnaire

1. *Your son, who is at medical school, telephones to say he can't take the stress any more and is leaving. You have spent a lot of money financing him, and endless energy supporting him both emotionally and practically. Do you:*
a) Feel his life will be a failure, and that you have failed as a parent because you should have been able to be a greater source of support to him?
b) Express regret and sadness, but let him know that you will stand by him whatever happens?
c) Feel it's his loss, but also feel angry and resentful about the money, time, and effort that has been wasted?

2. *Your best friend has asked you to help her stay away from her abusive boyfriend. You have housed her, comforted her, and encouraged her to go to the police. Then you discover that they are back together. Do you:*
a) Decide that you will never have anything more to do with her?
b) Meet her after work, beg her not to carry on her relationship with him, and insist that she come home with you now?
c) Tell her calmly when she telephones you that you will be there for her if she needs you, but you cannot stand by and watch her let herself be abused again?

3. *Although he has a long-standing alcohol problem, your husband insists on driving the car when he goes out in the evening. One night he crashes it, and, although he is not arrested, has damaged municipal property. He then blames you for not preventing him from driving. Do you:*
a) Agree that you should have stopped him, and pay for the damage?
b) Report him to the police for drunk driving?
c) Provide some information on an alcoholics' support group and statistics on road deaths caused by alcohol, telling him he is in serious danger of ruining your marriage as well as killing himself or someone else, and that if he does not get help you will leave him?

4. *When your partner does not get a new job she really wanted, she blames you—on the grounds that you have not been supportive enough about her career. Do you:*
a) Talk it through with another member of the family to try to determine if there is any truth in the statement before you respond?
b) Think that she is frustrated and looking for a scapegoat, and that she didn't get the job because she simply wasn't good enough?
c) Let her have a go at you, because you don't know what else you can do?

5. *One of your colleagues forgot to set the alarm in the shop where you both work. The shop is burgled, and your colleague is trying to persuade you to share the blame. Your job is definitely on the line. Do you:*

a) Wring your hands, and agree that you didn't notice that the alarm wasn't set when you left for the day?

b) Become outraged, and tell your colleague that he is incompetent and lazy—you're only surprised that he hasn't been found out before?

c) Firmly state that the job of setting the alarm was not part of your duties?

6. *One night in the middle of a furious argument, your boyfriend hits you. He says it is your fault, that you provoked him and made him lose his temper. Do you:*

a) Call on one of your brothers to respond with further violence?

b) Agree with him, knowing that some of your behavior can be infuriating, and that you obviously must have pushed him too far?

c) Finish with him then and there, saying that violence is never the victim's fault, and that you will not tolerate being treated like that?

7. *You discover that your wife has been having an affair for the past few years, although it is now over. She says she wants to make a fresh start with you and will commit herself to improving your marriage. Do you:*

a) Decide to end the relationship and insist on starting divorce proceedings, feeling that there is no way you could ever forgive her?

b) Feel devastated and betrayed, not knowing what you had done to make her do this, and thinking you are a useless lover and husband?

c) Agree to start counseling together so you can see where the relationship went wrong, and, although you are very upset, remain hopeful that you may be able to forge a new and better relationship together?

Conclusions

Now check your answers against the scores below and add up the total:

1. a) 3   **b)** 2   **c)** 1
2. a) 1   **b)** 3   **c)** 2
3. a) 3   **b)** 1   **c)** 2
4. a) 2   **b)** 1   **c)** 3
5. a) 3   **b)** 1   **c)** 2
6. a) 1   **b)** 3   **c)** 2
7. a) 1   **b)** 3   **c)** 2

If you scored **16–21**, you are too quick to feel responsible for resolving everyone else's crises. Realize that others must be allowed to make their own choices, and their own mistakes. If you take on too much, you may become overstressed yourself.

If you scored **10–15**, you know where the boundaries are between you and others, and do not try to take on more than you can handle. You usually allow those around you to take responsibility for their own crisis.

If you scored **9** points or under, you show a tendency to abandon people when the going gets tough. Sometimes this is appropriate—for example, if they are being violent—but in some cases, you may simply appear unsupportive and indifferent. By getting involved, you will develop a sense of responsibility, learn new strategies for coping, and become closer to the people around you.

Finding a way out

If you become overinvolved in someone else's crisis, you may start to feel trapped; drawing a boundary between your own and others' responsibilities gives you the freedom to take charge of your own life.

LISTEN TO YOUR BODY

MOST CRISES make demands on your body as well as your mind, but because you're probably focusing on strategies to cope with your problem, you may easily miss or ignore signs that you are becoming run down. If you don't recognize and act on these warning signals, such as chronic or intense headaches or persistent fatigue, your body is likely to break down, and you will become ill. This is, of course, the very last thing you need when dealing with a crisis.

To cope with a crisis, your body and brain need to be in tip-top condition, so you will reap enormous dividends if you regularly take stock of your physical well-being. By learning how to listen to your body and hear the warning signals, you can take the necessary remedial action before any symptoms worsen.

Make time for yourself

Try to plan your day so that you have at least 10 minutes to review your physical condition. Lunchtime, the end of the afternoon, or just before you go to bed are probably the most convenient times. Choose a quiet place where you can lie down comfortably and straighten your spine. Trying not to rush, take a few deep abdominal breaths (see "Learn to Relax," pp. 120-121); gentle, measured breathing is the best way to prepare you for deep relaxation so that you can listen to your body. Then, beginning with your head or your feet, focus on each part of your body in sequence. You may need to try a few times

before you feel you are able to be properly attentive to what your body is telling you, but by performing this exercise regularly, you will find immediate relief from tension, and you will be less likely to fall ill when under pressure.

Physical exercise is also a great way to relieve tension and to stay healthy. If you don't already exercise regularly, plan to make time to do so; even a quiet walk for 15 to 20 minutes a day is quite beneficial physically, and will also help to clear your mind.

Focus on your stomach
Stress, often due to unexpressed emotions such as fear or anger, may cause your stomach to churn so that you lose your appetite or perhaps binge on "comfort foods" such as ice cream. Taking slow, deep breaths may help.

Focus on your lower abdomen
Cramps are a definite sign of stress, and may indicate that your feelings are confused or bottled up. You may find relief by deep breathing.

Focus on your legs
Do they ache and feel tense? Perhaps you feel "unsupported" or long to run away from your problems. Contract and release the muscles, then let your legs rest against the floor.

Focus on your feet
If you stand most of the day, your feet may hurt. Rotate them gently, then stretch them by pointing your toes, then relax.

Focus on your lungs

If you are anxious, your breathing may be shallow and rapid, and you may feel tired. Breathe in slowly, and with each exhalation, imagine that you are releasing tension and anxiety.

Focus on your neck

A stiff, painful neck may reflect fatigue or an inflexible approach to your problem. Gently move your head from side to side.

Focus on your head

A headache may be due to tension or worries. Close your eyes and imagine your mind is like a peaceful, still lake.

Focus on your eyes

Do they ache? The message may be that you can't "see" any answers and are tired from looking so hard. Close your eyes, look up, down, and side to side, then let your eye muscles relax.

Focus on your jaw

If it is tight, it may be that you are repressing anger or negative emotions. Gently move your jaw to release any tension.

Focus on your shoulders

If they ache or are stiff, you may be working hard to protect yourself. Gently rotate only your shoulders, not your arms, in small circles, then let them rest against the floor.

Focus on your heart

A fast beat often indicates anxiety. Breathe slowly and deeply, and with each breath repeat to yourself, "I am calm and strong."

Focus on your arms

Do they ache? You may have over-exerted yourself, or perhaps are holding back pent-up energy. Gently stretch and release the muscles.

Focus on your wrists

Your wrists may ache if you work on a computer, or, like a stiff neck, this may indicate inflexibility. Gently rotate them clockwise, then anti-clockwise.

Focus on your hands

They may be sweaty and cold if you are tense, or perhaps they ache because you have been clenching them in anger. Make a tight fist, then stretch out your fingers. Then let your hands relax completely.

FOCUS AND RELEASE

Learn how to read your own body language by following the process outlined here.

These suggestions are not rigid, but are designed to prompt you to become aware of how your body feels. After focusing, there are simple exercises that you can use to relieve the immediate or more obvious tensions.

You may want to learn deeper relaxation techniques, and there are tapes, books, or classes that are designed for this purpose.

LEARN TO RELAX

Learning to relax is good for you, particularly when your body is reacting to the stress of a crisis and your sleep patterns are disturbed. A daily session of relaxation can help to repair the damage of the day and reduce stress levels by calming your mind, soothing away anxiety, refreshing your body, and restoring your energy.

There are many types of formal relaxation exercises, such as yoga or meditation, that you can learn; you can also use the techniques described here, putting them into practice right away.

Take a deep breath

The following technique, which is called abdominal (or diaphragmatic) breathing, can be used anywhere, and at any time of day, to reduce tension and promote tranquility. It should take only a few minutes to feel the benefits.

Start by lying on the floor. Put one hand just on or above your waist so that you can feel your diaphragm rise and fall as you breathe. Now just breathe in and out normally. Does your diaphragm push out before your ribs when you breathe in? If not, keep practicing until you feel your abdomen first and then your upper chest. It may take a little while to get the hang of it. Once you are used to it, stand in front of a mirror to check that your upper chest and shoulders do not move too much as you inhale.

Taking just one deep abdominal breath at the first sign of tension—when you are disturbed by an unwanted interruption, for example—can help reduce your feelings of stress, and leave you more able to think clearly and thus cope effectively.

Often, when you're under pressure, you'll find that your breathing starts to become quick and shallow, with the result that you may feel tired, anxious, and occasionally even dizzy. Diaphragmatic breathing is a simple and helpful way to remedy this, and to release any body tension.

Basic relaxation technique

Once you have mastered this deep, diaphragmatic breathing, you can try this simple relaxation technique; you can do it standing, sitting, or lying down—whichever you find most comfortable. Find a quiet place where you won't be disturbed.

• Breathe in through your nose for a count of four. Watch your diaphragm rise and relax your stomach muscles so that the breath reaches down into your abdomen.

• Hold your breath, and count slowly to four.

• Release your breath slowly and evenly through your mouth while counting to four.

• Repeat this sequence several times—preferably for up to ten minutes, which should enable you to reach a state of deep relaxation. Both your body and mind will benefit from the restorative powers of this simple technique.

Let yourself float
Picturing soothing images is another technique conducive to deep relaxation, permitting a respite from overfocusing on problems.

Get it taped

You may find it helpful to make a recording of the deep-breathing exercise so that your own voice guides the exercise and you do not have to think at all. You could record tapes of different length for use at different times, or add a slightly rousing end so that you don't fall asleep. Once you become familiar with the whole sequence, you may dispense with the spoken part and prefer to listen to soothing music—or you may discover that the exercise is more relaxing when you enjoy complete, restful silence.

Deeper relaxation

Once you have mastered abdominal breathing, you may want to learn other deep-relaxation techniques, perhaps by joining a class on meditation. Whatever you decide, your perseverance will be well rewarded.

DEEP RELAXATION

To have a session of deep relaxation, choose a time and place where you will not be disturbed. Take the phone off the hook. Sit or lie down with your spine straight, and your head and/or knees cushioned. Close your eyes, take a few abdominal breaths and follow the sequence described below.

• Concentrate on your feet and toes. Contract the muscles as tightly as you can for a few seconds, then relax and say to yourself (or record on tape), "My feet and toes are now completely relaxed."

• Repeat exactly the same sequence for the rest of your body, moving from your feet and toes to your calves, thighs, buttocks, stomach muscles, chest, hands, arms, shoulders, neck, jaw, and face. Feel the tension leaving each part of your body, as you repeat each time, "My (hands, arms, face, etc.) are now completely relaxed."

• Pause for a couple of minutes.

• Concentrate on your abdominal breathing for a couple of breaths.

• Pause again for a few moments.

• Now scan your body for any tension, and repeat the tension-hold-relax sequence if required.

• Clear your mind and feel the issues of the day drifting away. If worries from the day come up, simply notice them and let them go. Don't struggle to block out thoughts; just let your mind float.

• Imagine yourself at the top of a tall building. Visualize an escalator that is going to take you, at your own speed, to the basement. Imagine yourself descending. In the basement is your dream setting (such as a deserted beach, a beautiful garden, or a quiet room—whatever you choose). As you enter, tell yourself that you are going to lie down for five minutes in perfect peace. Lie down and let go.

• When you are ready to re-emerge—either at will or prompted by the end of your tape—take a breath, stretch gently, and slowly turn your attention to your surroundings; first become aware of the floor or chair beneath you, for example, then register any sounds or smells, then open your eyes and look around you. Slowly bring yourself up to a sitting position.

RELEASING TENSION

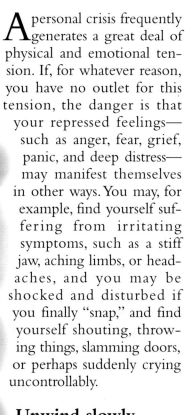

A personal crisis frequently generates a great deal of physical and emotional tension. If, for whatever reason, you have no outlet for this tension, the danger is that your repressed feelings—such as anger, fear, grief, panic, and deep distress—may manifest themselves in other ways. You may, for example, find yourself suffering from irritating symptoms, such as a stiff jaw, aching limbs, or headaches, and you may be shocked and disturbed if you finally "snap," and find yourself shouting, throwing things, slamming doors, or perhaps suddenly crying uncontrollably.

Unwind slowly

To maintain your well-being and to minimize the potentially harmful physical effects of stress (see "The Body Under Pressure," pp. 92-93), it is important that you find an outlet so you can release tension in a controlled way. By doing so, you may also discover an added benefit: Once you are no longer so obsessed by your problems, your mind will become clearer, and you will be more likely to find the best solution.

Time to unwind
There are two important factors that will help you to unwind and release tension: giving yourself a break, and finding an appropriate outlet.

FINDING AN OUTLET

You are far more likely to manage a crisis effectively if you feel physically fit and can maintain a sense of proportion about your problems. There are many things you can do to help yourself.

Emotional safety valves
The techniques listed below will help you reduce the risk of an uncontrolled emotional outburst.
• **Laughter** is great medicine, so watch your favorite television comedy, treat yourself to a funny film, and let yourself go and have a good laugh.
• **Weeping** can be therapeutic, and a movie or book that moves you to tears is often the best way to express feelings you might be hiding.
• **Shouting and screaming** at a football match or a pop concert is an opportunity to express your frustrations and vent strong feelings in safety.
• **Pummeling a pillow** is another good way to express the anger you might feel you have to hide.
• **Writing about your situation** is an excellent way to clarify your thoughts about your dilemma. Keeping a confidential diary can be an important safety valve, as is writing a not-to-be-sent letter to someone who may be involved in or partly responsible for your crisis. Writing enables you to release tension by being honest about your feelings, and helps put your situation in perspective.

Exercise is best
Physical activity is an excellent way to release both physical and mental tension. Whatever form of exercise you choose to do, remember that it is always best to increase fitness levels gradually. Among those that are particularly good for releasing tension are:
• **Swimming.** You might try to swim as fast as you can for a couple of laps to warm up, and then slow down gradually before continuing at a more measured pace; try to swim for about 20 minutes.

• **Running.** If you are fit, a short sprint can help loosen tense or aching leg muscles. A brisk jog or fast walk can be just as effective for those who are less fit.

• **Walking or cycling.** Either exercise is a great way to relieve stress. Incorporate a walk or cycle ride into your daily routine, such as your journey to and from work, to help clear your mind. Start at a brisk speed, then slow down to a gentler, steady pace.

Let yourself go
Even ordinary household tasks can be an outlet for pent-up energy.

• **Stairwalking.** This exercise helps to relieve the stiffness that may occur if you sit at a desk most of the day, and provides a mental break from work.

• **Hitting or throwing a ball.** Any exercise that incorporates these activities is a wonderful way to release tension in the arms and shoulders.

• **Gardening and home improvements.** Provided that these activities are not stressful, and that you do not put yourself under pressure by imposing a strict deadline, they can help ease stiffness and tension, offer a relief from your preoccupations, and contribute to a sense of achievement.

• **Dancing.** Letting go completely to a favorite piece of music will almost certainly leave you feeling better. Music is a great mood-lifter.

• **Massage.** Although not precisely "exercise," massage eases tense muscles and joints, and will leave you feeling pampered and relaxed.

Try to achieve a balance between strenuous exercises, which release tension and provide a surge of invigorating oxygen to your muscles and brain, and gentler, more sustained exercises, which will improve your stamina, suppleness, and general fitness. You might want to swim for half an hour one day and walk for an hour the next, or perhaps run for 15-30 minutes three times a week and do yoga or other stretching exercises on the weekends.

Apart from the benefit of feeling better equipped to face problems, exercise is also a way to look better, thereby enhancing your self-image. In addition, exercise promotes the production of endorphins, substances found mainly in the brain; these not only are the body's natural painkillers, but also promote a feeling of well-being. Finally, exercise will help you sleep better—which is often difficult during a crisis—and will ensure you're rested enough to cope.

BUILD UP YOUR STRENGTH

E ating sensibly is probably the last thing on your mind when you are in the thick of a crisis. You may feel that you just don't have time to worry about eating and cooking properly, and, instead, crave "comfort" foods, such as cakes, chocolate, or ice cream, that are not really nutritious and are high in fats and sugar. The problem with this is that the instant gratification you may derive from eating them is often soon replaced by a drop in energy, possible weight gain, and a loss of self-esteem—all of which merely adds to your difficulties.

Emotional stress always involves physical stress (see "The Body Under Pressure," pp. 92–93). Your body responds by sending extra blood to the muscles—which is part of the fight-or-flight response of heightened arousal due to the "danger" of your crisis. This often leaves the vital organs less well supplied with oxygen and therefore less efficient. Poor functioning of the digestive system, for example, is a particularly common symptom of stress.

Tempt yourself

Even when you don't feel like it, it is important that you eat regularly during a crisis. If your stomach is empty all the time, you are more likely to suffer from indigestion or lack of energy, and, in extreme circumstances, could end up with an ulcer. Try to make your meals small, light, and tempting, including enough food rich in carbohydrates (such as potatoes and wholegrain bread and pasta) to help sustain your energy, rather than relying on sugary snacks. Make the food pleasing to look at, and try to create an attractive ambience in which to eat by having fresh flowers on the table. Take the time to enjoy the meal you've prepared, and see it as the part of the day when you can relax.

Buy the most delicious seasonal produce you can find, occasionally treat yourself to luxurious fruits and vegetables, and add herbs, fruit, or nuts to mixed leaves to create appetizing, attractive salads.

If you are under pressure and feeling miserable, it is best to treat your body carefully. A healthy diet will ensure a healthy body and a better state of mind, leaving you better equipped to cope in a crisis. If you consider the care you take with your meals as a way of pampering yourself, it will provide the occasional break you need during a crisis.

Balance your diet
Proper nutrition, without too much junk food, ensures that you will have enough energy reserves to cope during a crisis.

Drinking lots of water and fresh fruit juice will help flush away toxins in your system. Recommended daily water consumption is four pints (about two liters), so try keeping a bottle with you to sip from regularly. Drink about eight ounces (about 250ml) of low-fat milk each day, or take it with breakfast cereal. Avoid or limit your consumption of tea, coffee, and cola: They contain caffeine, which may overstimulate you (sometimes causing tremors) and only add to the tension you are already feeling. Although alcohol is believed to relax some people, it also tends to have a depressing effect, and so is best avoided or drunk only in moderation.

Plan to eat at least one balanced meal each day, choosing foods that are easily digested, and aim to eat five or six portions of fresh fruit and vegetables daily. Also, try to avoid fried foods. Substitute poached, steamed, or grilled food as much as possible, and limit your intake of butter and cream.

If you tend to eat between meals, try to have tasty but healthy snacks readily available, such as sticks or slices of raw vegetables, including carrots, celery, courgettes, mushrooms, peppers, and cauliflower. You might eat these with a low-fat cheese or dip. Fresh fruit, low-fat yogurts, or a few nuts also make good snacks.

The more you look after your body, the healthier you will be, and the better you will feel about yourself and your ability to cope with your crisis.

GET FRESH

The first consideration is to maintain good nutrition and an adequate supply of vitamins and minerals. You can take vitamin supplements, but they are no real substitute for fresh food and meals you prepare yourself.

Vitamin B helps to convert food to energy, and is vital for the healthy functioning of the nervous system. It can be depleted more quickly when you are physically or mentally exhausted. Because clear thinking and adequate reserves of energy are crucial during any crisis, try to ensure that your diet includes plenty of Vitamin B, found in liver, whole grains, wholemeal bread, nuts, seeds, and pulses.

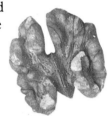

Vitamin C helps the body fight the effects of stress and boosts your immune system. All fresh fruit and vegetables contain Vitamin C, but citrus fruits, blackcurrants, strawberries, kiwi fruits, watercress, green peppers, raw cabbage, broccoli, cauliflower, spinach, and parsley are rich in this nutrient.

Protein and calcium maintain strong muscles and bones. Meat, fish, nuts, pulses, and eggs all provide protein, while all dairy products and sesame seeds are an excellent source of calcium.

YOUR INNER WISDOM

LIKE EVERYONE ELSE, you probably have a little voice inside your head, commenting on what you observe or do throughout the day, or perhaps giving you advice. This voice, sometimes called "self-talk," is the most obvious facet of your inner or subconscious thoughts, and plays a vital role when you have to cope with a crisis. Sometimes your inner voice will sound like your best friend, encouraging you to take care of yourself, but it can also be your worst enemy, telling you how useless you are so that you fail at a task before you begin.

Listen carefully

If you have a positive self-image, your self-talk is likely to reflect this, and so enhance your potential for successful decision-making. Many people, however, suffer from low self-esteem, and the voice they hear is critical: a barrage of defeatist self-talk that leaves them ill-equipped to see their situations clearly.

If your inner voice is like this, dealing with any difficult problem will probably be extremely stressful: You may be afraid to make decisions, and the ones you do make may well be unsatisfactory. See if you can hear your inner voice, and then ask yourself these questions:

• **What exactly is the message of your voice?**
If your inner voice is a stream of negative messages, try "reframing" them; for example, if your inner voice says, "If I do this, everyone will know my business," have the voice say something like, "If I do this, people will get to know me better, and I'll feel closer to them."

Your inner tape
You can enhance your ability to meet life's challenges by ensuring that your inner "self-talk" tape is a positive one.

• Who is speaking?

You can change your inner voice if you can identify the speaker. For example, your inner voice might say, "I don't like swimming," but it may echo your mother saying, "I'm afraid of the water."

• Is your inner voice intrusive?

If your "self-talk" never stops, imagine that the voice is coming from a radio or television, and simply turn down the volume.

• What is the tone of the voice?

If your inner voice sounds aggressive, harshly loud, whiny, or complaining, try making it gentler or quieter, or more assertive.

A new tool for change

During a crisis, you may be more fearful and self-critical than usual, and these feelings may be reinforced by critical, nagging self-talk. Your inner voice may also be so relentless that you are unable to think clearly, which contributes to indecision.

No matter how your inner voice sounds or what it says, it is one of the most powerful tools you have to help you cope with a crisis. It is also within your power to modify it, so that instead of being an enemy that undermines you, it becomes a wise companion, one that will help you achieve your goals and enhance your life.

RECORD A NEW SCRIPT

If your inner voice is endlessly criticizing you, debating small points, or reminding you of past failures, you will not be in the best shape when you have to face a crisis. You can, however, erase the old tape and record a new one.

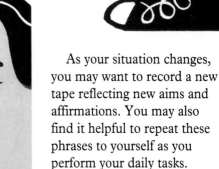

• First, write a new script that will help you deal positively with any problem you are facing. You might write statements such as, "I can deal with this effectively. I have faith in my abilities." Include precise details, such as the desired outcome, dates, and the names of anyone involved. The most effective scripts are those that are the most personal.

• Record the script, putting your energy into sounding optimistic and highly motivated, yet natural. This exercise is most beneficial when you hear your own voice because you will identify with it more strongly. Make several recordings, then choose the one you like most.

• Choose a quiet time of the day when you will not be interrupted, and listen to your tape. Don't rush: If you listen to this tape in peace and quiet, preferably after a relaxation session (see "Learn to Relax," pp. 120-121), the positive messages will slowly but surely reach your subconscious. Gradually, the character of your inner voice will become more positive, thus changing your self-image and enhancing your self-confidence.

As your situation changes, you may want to record a new tape reflecting new aims and affirmations. You may also find it helpful to repeat these phrases to yourself as you perform your daily tasks.

PICTURE YOURSELF COPING

Think of your subconscious as a vast personal library. The dreams and daydreams generated by this resource are full of images, sounds, and sensations—and indeed, they sometimes even hold the vital answers to your most troublesome problems.

Why we dream

Dreams are an important source of our identity: Everyone has a unique history, and no-one else will ever have a dream exactly like yours. Dreams are efforts to sift and sort out experiences, your attempts to understand what has occurred and perhaps view a situation from a different perspective. Sometimes, they may be rehearsals for what is likely to occur if you pursue a particular course of action.

After a crisis, such as an illness, a car accident, a mugging, or a burglary, you may find yourself suffering recurring dreams or nightmares. This is your mind's attempt to assimilate what may be a radical

change in circumstances. Keeping a dream journal can help you chart your progress, and provide insights into your subconscious thoughts.

Guiding your dreams

Research into sleep patterns has revealed that dreams may sometimes be consciously influenced by pre-sleep directions; for example, just before going to sleep, think of the problem for which you need a solution, and then say to yourself, "My dream will provide me with an answer." Because your brain never really sleeps, your subconscious mind, acting on your suggestion, may generate helpful images or words that are still with you when you wake up, so keep a notepad by the bed.

Guided affective imagery (GAI)

You can also "talk" to your subconscious by relaxing and letting images or daydreams "speak to you." Try the following exercise, known as guided affective imagery (GAI):

- Find a quiet place where you will not be disturbed, and make yourself comfortable.
- Wearing comfortable clothes, lie down, close your eyes, and then relax fully (see "Learn to Relax," pp. 120-121).
- Imagine a landscape. Allow your mind's eye to wander freely around this landscape, exploring it thoroughly. Don't try too hard or force your impressions; instead, let them carry you along. If you find that other thoughts are distracting you from your exploration, don't worry. Let these thoughts come and go; with time and practice, they will become less intrusive.
- Ask yourself questions about this landscape. Is it a rocky mountain, or a sunlit, flower-filled meadow? Is it a desert, a garden, or a forest? Are there any buildings? Are there any people or animals? What are your feelings about them, and what is your relationship with them? Are you in this landscape, and if so, what are you doing?

WHY IMAGES ARE EFFECTIVE

There are three main benefits to having a dialogue with your subconscious through images:

• **You can understand more about your personality.** Are you stable and on top of things, or fearful and unable to deal with any crisis, large or small? Are you confused and indecisive? The types of images that "speak to you" will give you an idea of your self-image, helping you estimate your strength and build a firm foundation.

• **You can gain an insight into what underlies past or present problems.** A traumatic past incident buried in your subconscious may resurface as a compelling image, illuminating the possible roots of your dilemma and why you react the way you do.

• **You can develop strategies for coping with crises.** Imagining yourself succeeding is a non-threatening dress rehearsal for you to experience the positive benefits of overcoming a difficult situation.

What the images mean

In her book *Positive Thinking*, Vera Peiffer describes the conclusions from the GAI landscape exercise with clients. She believes that an open, flowery meadow is an indication of a stable personality, whereas a stretch of scrubby grass, surrounded by tall hedges, indicates fears and inhibitions. Animals that are dangerous may signal that a person could be facing a very difficult situation, whereas friendly ones could embody the qualities needed to bring the situation to a successful resolution.

Lucky charms

Because images are symbolic representations of subconscious problems, you can choose any image you like to help you solve a problem, not just a landscape. Different images will work in different situations. Amusing or silly images can be quite effective: hypnotherapists who deal with phobias think that getting people to laugh at what they fear is helpful, and suggest that someone who is afraid of spiders visualize them as dressed in a ridiculous outfit.

Once you have found images that help you to deal with your problems, think of them as your personal lucky charms. The next time you find yourself under stress in some way, take a deep, relaxing breath, and focus on your personal positive images for a few minutes to calm yourself.

Remember that if something symbolizes or evokes reality for you, then it can be every bit as meaningful as "real life."

Open the doors to your mind
Guided affective imagery, as well as dreams, can be a gateway to your problem—and its resolution.

CHECK YOUR BELIEFS

How you deal with crises is a product of what you believe about yourself, about others, and about the world around you. Think back over any crises that have occurred in your life, both major and minor. Can you remember how you coped—not just what practical action you took, but also how you felt about them emotionally? Is there a pattern to how you coped? Now think about what your beliefs are. Did they influence how you felt or acted? Was this influence mainly positive or negative? Perhaps it is time to examine or change some of your beliefs. According to practitioners of NLP (Neuro-Linguistic Programming), there is a basic hierarchy of "Logical Levels" on which people operate. In *Changing Belief Systems with NLP*, author Robert Dilts describes this as follows:

Level A: My identity
Level B: My beliefs
Level C: My capabilities
Level D: My behavior and actions
Level E: My reactions

Dilts explains how changes in the basic assumptions expressed in the upper levels (A and B) can filter through to those below. The example below illustrates how someone suffering from a serious illness might have either of two very different approaches:

Negative approach
Level A: I am a victim of a serious illness.
Level B: I must accept the inevitable.
Level C: I am unable to stay well.
Level D: I have many symptoms of (the illness).
Level E: (The illness) is destroying me.

You can see how such self-limiting beliefs would undermine a person's will to get well.

Positive approach
Level A: I am basically a healthy person.
Level B: If I am healthy, I can help other people with the same illness.
Level C: I can influence how healthy I am by choosing appropriate treatment to heal myself.
Level D: I can at least behave like a healthy person whenever possible.
Level E: The treatment is healing me.

Do your beliefs help or hinder you?

This questionnaire will help you find out if your beliefs help you cope in a crisis—or make you more likely to feel overwhelmed. If you "usually" agree with a belief below, score 1 point; if "often," score 2; if "sometimes," score 3; if "never," score 4. Finally, add up your score, then read the conclusions at the end of the quiz.

As the crisis looms...

1. I know I won't have the confidence/strength/skills/intelligence to deal with this properly.
2. All I can do is sit back, watch events unfold, and let things take their course.
3. I feel that something awful is going to happen, but I have no idea what, which makes me feel much worse.
4. If I just carry on as if everything is all right, maybe the crisis will pass.
5. I can feel panic setting in and my self-control slipping away.
6. I'm beginning to get feelings just like when I was a child, and _____ happened to me and I felt miserable and powerless.
7. This will be just like the time when _____ occurred and that turned out really badly.

During the crisis...
1. I've brought this on myself again, and it's all my fault—will I never learn?
2. Everyone is so unsympathetic.
3. No-one can possibly understand how I feel.
4. Why me? One disaster after another happens to me. Other people have a much easier time.
5. It doesn't matter what I do, what will be, will be—that's life. It's probably just my destiny to suffer when things go wrong.
6. Will this nightmare never end?
7. One minute one course of action seems best, then the next minute, I think I should do the opposite. I don't know which way to turn.
8. I wish someone else would decide for me.
9. I'm just not someone who copes well in a crisis.
10. This has happened to me because I'm being paid back for the time that I behaved badly/was unkind or cruel, etc.

After the crisis
1. I've struggled through this time; I just hope nothing like this ever happens again.
2. What does everybody think about how I coped? I bet I made a fool of myself.
3. I knew I would deal with it badly, just like I always do, and I did.
4. What I should have done is...
5. What terrible thing is going to happen next? They say that lots of disasters tend to happen one after another.
6. It wasn't really much of a crisis, I just made too much fuss about it and didn't nip it in the bud. Most other people probably wouldn't have viewed it as a problem at all.
7. This experience has scarred me forever.

Conclusions
24-48: Low self-esteem makes you feel powerless or doomed to fail when facing problems. These beliefs work as self-fulfilling prophecies. Work at altering your beliefs and establishing greater self-esteem so that you start to see yourself as a capable person who is able to choose the right course of action and learn from the experience.

49-72: You value your abilities to cope quite highly, but should work on raising your self-esteem so that, instead of thinking "I'll get through somehow," you believe "I can deal with this very effectively." Don't attach too much value to what others think, and don't lose faith in yourself halfway through.

73-96: Your beliefs carry you through with a positive attitude. You usually take control from the start and do what you can to improve a situation. But don't believe yourself to be invincible—you are allowed to be less than perfect, and you don't always have to cope alone.

Give yourself the thumbs up
Having a positive attitude and believing in yourself can help you act more effectively in a crisis; you will be able to respond flexibly and creatively.

ASKING FOR HELP

ONE OF THE MOST DISTRESSING aspects of going through a crisis is how isolated it can make you feel. You may be so confused that you simply cannot discuss your feelings, or frightened that, if you do say anything, you will feel embarrassed. You may also fear being thought of as weak and inadequate. But keeping things to yourself can actually make them worse. When a problem is on your mind all the time, it is hard to think clearly, and you may end up convinced that only the worst can happen.

Sharing your thoughts

There are many therapeutic benefits in talking things over. First, once you have been brave enough to speak about your problem, you will find that its significance has almost instantly diminished. As soon as you share it with someone on your side, you are no longer alone and isolated.

To understand the importance of sharing worries with those closest to you, imagine how you would feel if your best friend told you that she had been going through a very difficult time but could not tell you. You might be distressed that she was going through a crisis on her own when you would have been happy to help, but you might also be hurt by the implied lack of trust, and loss of

closeness. If she were not being honest in this context, you may question whether she was being honest in other aspects of your relationship.

While you might not want to burden a close friend with the pain you are feeling, you could be doing both of you a disservice. Many good relationships have been destroyed by one partner going through a crisis, such as bereavement, but failing to talk to the other partner, who then feels rejected. Your family and close friends will almost certainly sense when something is wrong. Without knowing the truth, they may well imagine the worst and will worry anyway. Let them know the truth, even if you don't want to go into too much detail, and ask for their support and understanding. They will then not feel excluded or rejected.

If your work is affected, either from a need for extra time off or because you cannot concentrate, you are better off explaining to your employer, rather than waiting until you are hauled in for lateness or poor work. Most companies are sympathetic to reasonable requests for support during difficult times; some even provide counseling.

Choosing your confidant

If you would feel happier going over the details of your problem with someone who is not intimately involved in your life—perhaps because he or she may be able to make valuable, impartial observations that you, in your unsettled state, might have

---

IT'S GOOD TO TALK

Talking about your problems can help you:

• Reduce your fear of the problem
• Increase your understanding
• Find out how the crisis arose in the first place
• Release pent-up feelings
• Work out how you really feel
• Learn how others feel about the crisis
• Get support when you're feeling isolated
• Strengthen relationships with those you talk to
• Feel reassured
• Get new ideas and a different perspective on the problem and how to resolve it
• Discover solutions and assess their feasibility.

overlooked—then you should talk to a professional, such as a doctor, therapist, or counselor. A support group or self-help organization that deals specifically with your particular problem may offer the sort of help you want. Libraries, your doctor's office, and advice centers usually offer lists of support groups. Whoever you choose to talk to, it is important that you feel comfortable. If you don't, you can always change your counselor or group.

Getting together

Even if your chosen confidant is not a professional—perhaps simply a wise close friend—make an appointment to get together, and give them some idea of what you want to talk about. Try to choose a suitable environment, and allow yourself enough time to explore the matter fully. It may take a while to organize your thoughts, and it will not help if you

have to abandon your discussions just when you feel comfortable or solutions seem apparent.

It is a good idea to think about what sort of response you think you want from people with whom you decide to share your problem. You may simply need someone to listen, sympathize, and discuss the ideas you already have to solve it. Their support, however, often gives you confidence to implement your decisions.

You will find that people love you just as much when you have problems as when you don't. You're still the same person; it's just the things that are happening to you that have changed. Sharing your problems can often improve your relationships, help solve your problems, and will certainly leave you feeling stronger and no longer isolated.

Get support
Reaching out to someone else—whether a friend, a professional, or a telephone advice service—can give you the support you need.

FINDING SUPPORT

If you are in the thick of a crisis, or dealing with the aftermath of one, you may be well aware that you desperately need help and support, but feel uncertain as to what help you need, or where to find it. Acknowledging that you want help is an important first step. You then need to ask yourself the following questions:

• *What exactly is the nature of my problem*? For example, is it a clear-cut, short-term problem, or an underlying difficulty with long-term implications?

• *What kind of help do I need*? Do I need emotional support and companionship—just someone to "be there" for me—or do I need information, advice, and practical know-how?

• *Who would I prefer to talk to*? Would I feel embarrassed if I talked to a family member, and, if so, would the objectivity offered by a professional adviser of some sort be more appropriate/helpful?

Using these guidelines, you can begin to formulate your plan of action and set out in search of the appropriate help you need.

The search begins

You probably know who you can call on in the way of family, friends, and work colleagues, but, if you decide you need professional support, consider the full range of help that falls under that heading. Depending on the crisis, you might want to turn to your doctor, a citizens' advice bureau, the social services department, a psychotherapist or counselor, or a psychiatrist.

There are other professionals who may have a role to play in many problems, including teachers, alternative health practitioners, lawyers, and police officers; you might contact a particular professional simply to get some basic information about, for example, your health or your rights. It is important to remember that some problems may need different types of help from different sources. An alcoholic, for example, might well need all of the following:

• Emotional support and encouragement from family, close friends, and work colleagues

• Medical help from a doctor and/or guidance from a psychologist to uncover the root causes of the addiction

• Long-term practical advice and understanding from a support group such as Alcoholics Anonymous, where experiences can be shared with others who have had similar difficulties.

Well supported
As well as asking for help and support when you need it, whether from a partner, family members, friends, or professionals, you may have to learn how to accept it, and trust that people care about you.

The self-help network

There is an enormous range of voluntary advice centers, telephone helplines, and support or self-help groups so that people can come to terms with all types of trauma, such as bereavement, cancer, unemployment, rape, losing a child, alcoholism, drug abuse, and gambling. Groups range from informal or local discussion circles, where people derive great comfort, help, and support simply from being with others who share their experience in some way, to powerful, nationwide, high-profile organizations. Your local library, doctor, or social services department will often have more information. Also check self-help books that deal with the relevant topics, as these often list support groups at the back, or contact a well-known group dealing with a similar issue; they are usually familiar with all kinds of smaller groups. Alternatively, you may want to start your own group (see box, below).

Exploring some of these different avenues will help you define your problem more clearly so that it becomes easier to tackle. You will gain greater self-awareness, but the greatest benefit is that you will be advised of the solutions and strategies other people have found, which you can then adapt to help you in your current situation.

SETTING UP A SUPPORT GROUP

Even the smallest, most modest support group can be of enormous help to people who, for whatever reason, feel unable to cope with their problems on their own. If you want to set up your own group, the guidelines below may be helpful:

1. Decide on what scale you want the group to operate—do you want a small, informal discussion group in your home, or a group that could become a campaigning organization? How wide do you want to cast your net when it comes to offering help—for example, would you want to help people who have suffered any kind of physical or mental abuse, or one particular kind of abuse? Be clear about exactly why you are forming the group—if everyone has very different experiences, then it might not get far.

2. Decide whether you want to call on expert help. There are many highly effective groups run entirely *by* ordinary people *for* ordinary people, but you might want to consult a professional occasionally. Learn to recognize when you really need professional support—informal groups can very easily be overdominated by "experts."

3. How many people do you know already who might want to join or help in some way? Your friends, colleagues, and acquaintances may be able to offer help, and you could advertize in local papers both for assistance and for fellow sufferers.

4. Try contacting other self-help groups and voluntary organizations for advice, which could range from how to run discussions to issues surrounding legal and publicity matters.

5. No matter what action you take—whether it is helping a disabled person to shop or starting a political lobby—you must decide whether you are in a position to take on the responsibility. Your group should also establish a decision-making process; otherwise, nothing will get done and the group could fizzle out due to frustration.

HOPE IN CRISIS

The old saying "every cloud has a silver lining" may be the last thing you want to hear when you are in a crisis, but, like most clichés, it holds more than a grain of truth. Think back over your life: How many times has a difficult situation ultimately produced unexpected benefits?

Shifting perspectives

During a crisis, you may find yourself going through a period of intense self-examination as you drop your daily defenses and lay bare some of your deepest emotions and thoughts to those around you.

Dealing with problems, and coping with their aftermath, can increase self-knowledge, and bring you much closer to certain people: A personal bond forged during trying circumstances can be a very strong, long-lasting one.

A crisis may also cause you to re-evaluate the world around you, to change your perspective and priorities, and to redirect your life toward different aspirations. It may make you see the true value of friendship and so alter your attitude to people or to career goals. These benefits rarely seem clear while you are struggling to deal with your problems, but usually begin to emerge after the crisis has passed. You may already have experienced problems after which you looked back and said: "It wasn't really so bad—and at least I learned…."

In short, the only prerequisite you need for overcoming and even benefiting from a bad situation is keeping an open mind and as positive an outlook as possible.

Discovering hope

Even when you feel lost or uncertain of your direction, you may unexpectedly find your way again—perhaps an entirely new direction or sense of purpose.

REFRAMING YOUR EXPERIENCES

Your personal outlook—your sense of your own identity and general beliefs—can be changed from negative to positive, thereby enabling you to cope with a crisis more effectively. Practitioners of NLP (Neuro-Linguistic Programming) believe that we can

positively "reframe" our difficult experiences or even our negative self-image in a number of ways that are easy to learn. These strategies, some of which are discussed below, can make a difference during a crisis.

• **Finding new and more positive meanings for your feelings, behavior, and experiences.** For example, if you avoid one family member because seeing them reminds you of the death of a favorite relative, you might think: "Seeing this relative reminds me very powerfully of ——, which is good, because I have so many happy memories of great times we enjoyed together." Here, what is exchanged is a negative meaning that tries to suppress feelings for a more positive, expressive one.

• **Finding new, more appropriate contexts for your behavior.** This means finding the best arena in which to express yourself. For example, your family may resent the fact that you "organize everything," which they see as bullying, so you might redirect your energy by working for a cause that is close to your heart.

• **Using new or more positive words or expressions.** For example, a "worrying situation" becomes a "challenging experience," or "my girlfriend dumped me and my life is a mess" becomes "the relationship ended so I now have the chance to make a fresh start."

• **Distinguishing between "intention" and "behavior" and finding new, more appropriate behaviors to satisfy the same intention.** For example, if you want to help someone close who is going through a bad patch, simply listening as he or she tries to deal with a crisis may help more than offering your analysis of the predicament.

Daring to be positive

Shirley had failed to get exam results that were good enough for her to pursue her dream of studying law, and felt that her world had fallen apart. She had been doing a part-time job helping out at a local nursing home while preparing for a second attempt at the exam, and had been surprised at how much she had enjoyed the work. Several people there frequently commented on how good she was with people. When a permanent job came up at the home, a relative who worked for the social services department suggested that she might like to consider taking the post and doing evening classes in social work at the same time. As a result, Shirley found a new vocation for which she was much better suited, and began to see herself as a highly competent, professional, and sensitive caregiver rather than as a failed or mediocre lawyer.

Adam learned from his crisis when his wife left with their children and decided to divorce him. For months, life was unbearable, but in trying to work out the best possible future arrangements for the children, he and his wife arrived at an uneasy truce. Making a real effort to consider his children's needs brought Adam closer to them than he had ever been before. While bitterly regretting that such unhappy circumstances made him see that he had been an "absent father" in some ways, he also felt he had at least seen what went wrong while his children were still young—and resolved to rebuild and deepen his relationship with them.

Neither Shirley nor Adam knew how resilient they were, but their stories illustrate the fact that if you decide to tackle everything life has to offer with a positive attitude and optimism, then you can find hope anywhere—even during a crisis.

A Silver Lining

Although few of us would welcome a crisis, we know that many challenges bring out the best in us. A crisis always involves change and, although this can be unsettling or even alarming, change provides opportunities for growth and improvement: the chance to increase your insight into yourself, to become closer to others, and to look at your life afresh. At the very least, the silver lining of an unexpected dark cloud may be a new strength, which may be valuable in the future. The following key points should remind you that even the darkest crisis holds the possibility of a hidden benefit.

Becoming a parent

New parents can find the experience exhausting as well as enjoyable, and some mothers suffer from post-natal depression. It is not uncommon for the father to feel rejected and isolated because of the mother's especially close bond with her baby. Friends and family can offer vital emotional and practical support and may enjoy the chance to become more involved. Working out your own parenting strategies as a couple can bring you closer together.

Wedded bliss?

When the honeymoon's over, the less romantic realities of day-to-day life together can seem a let-down, particularly if you have had unrealistic expectations of unending bliss; sometimes people even wonder if they've made a big mistake. Learn to communicate about your feelings, concerns, and desires. Building a strong relationship takes work—but brings rich rewards.

Relationship in crisis?

Can you spot the warning signs when a crisis is looming? You can defuse problems before they become explosive by being aware of brewing difficulties, rather than trying to ignore them. Having the courage to face them with your partner, and learning to talk and negotiate to resolve conflict, will strengthen your relationship.

Divorce

Separating from your partner doesn't mean you have to resort to all-out war. If you can maintain mutual respect and continue to act as cooperative co-parents to your children, you will find that you both have the opportunity to grow and develop your separate lives rather than tying up your energy in agonizing about your loss and the past.

Off to work…
Starting a new job can be a daunting prospect and you may worry about failing or not fitting in. Never be afraid to ask for guidance; other people often welcome the chance to share their expertise and skills. Show your willingness to learn, and view the challenge as a series of opportunities to expand your capabilities and develop your potential.

Moving house
Even if you are moving to a larger house, a nicer area, or even your dream home, moving house can be stressful. The loss of friendly neighbors or of what is familiar can make you feel unstable and insecure. Being prepared for these feelings, and planning your move as well as you can, helps to reduce stress so that you can enjoy your new home.

Illness
A long or serious illness, whether it affects you or a loved one, can be debilitating and depressing. A positive mental attitude not only affects how you feel; in many cases, it can also aid recovery. Being forced to slow down can make you look at your life in a new way and appreciate the days of relative good health. Discovering you have the strength to cope also enhances your self-esteem.

Bereavement
When someone close to you dies, it can feel as if you will never be happy again. There are no short cuts to avoiding the inevitable emotional pain of a major loss, but bereaved people often find that their experience ultimately makes them cherish the joys that life has to offer. Because intimacy becomes more important, they become more open with their feelings. They also focus their energies on creating rewarding, fulfilling lives.

Coping with crime
If you are the victim of a crime, it can make you feel vulnerable, distraught, and angry. Joining a support group and taking appropriate practical action, such as signing up for a self-defense class, can help you feel more empowered and less victimized.

Out of work
Losing your job, or even facing retirement at the end of a long working life, can undermine your sense of security and identity. Some people find they feel valueless and suffer from lowered self-esteem. Using the time to develop a broader range of interests, or perhaps striking out in a new direction, can bring unexpected benefits.

COMMENTS AND ANALYSIS

Pages 32–33:
Check Your Relationship

Did you find that the questions that pointed up areas of conflict or frustration were largely concentrated in one area, such as sex or money? Persistent problems often seem to fall into one area only, but if they are not dealt with, they can start to have a negative influence on other aspects of the relationship, too. Resentment over a partner's irresponsible attitude toward money, for example, could spill over into your sex life. As you responded to the questions, perhaps you noticed how strongly you felt about each issue, and how seriously you viewed

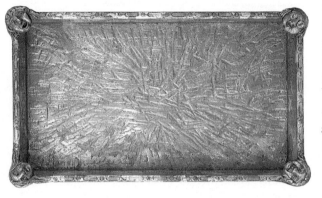

a particular problem. If you feel any of the problem areas could cause a crisis in your relationship, you and your partner might consider seeing a counselor.

Pages 96–97:
Good or Bad Stress?

You may have ticked a combination of positive and negative statements, but did you tick a greater number of statements in the beginning or latter part of each section? Read the conclusion for the statements that most apply to you.

At work
1–9: Positive. You're able to keep on top of things at work, and to turn potentially bad stress into good stress. You can leave the stress and tension of work behind you at the end of the day, and enjoy the other areas of your life.
10–18: Negative. You're probably under a lot of

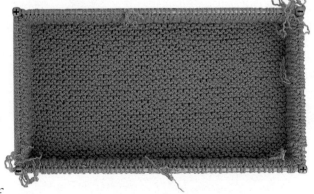

negative stress at work. The anger and frustration you often feel may be a direct result of your inability to assert yourself appropriately or to delegate tasks to others. Try to determine how you might be contributing to your own problems at work, and how you might change your behavior.

Relationships
1–8: Positive. You're able to get the support and help you need from those around you. You generally feel content and at peace with yourself and others, largely because you're able to express your needs and feelings easily.
9–16: Negative. You may be isolating yourself unnecessarily. You may often feel alone because you tend to withdraw or become introspective rather than to ask for help. You may also feel very envious of people who are able to have close, giving relationships. Think about how your view of yourself may be spoiling your chances for intimacy.

Physical health
1–9: Positive. You're generally in good health and are able to take care of yourself in a sensible, balanced way. You feel at ease in your body, use your good health to help you enjoy life, and would never be described as a hypochondriac.
10–21: Negative. It may be that you express your inner tension and stress through illness. Your choice not to care for yourself properly could reflect a lack of self-esteem. You may need to look beyond your physical ills to the deeper meaning of your conflicts and problems.

Creativity
1–10: Positive. You have the ability both to enjoy the creativity of others, such as by listening to music or looking at paintings, as well as to take full advantage of your own creative talents. You are probably mentally agile and quite good at lateral thinking—the ability to solve problems creatively by taking an unusual or unexpected approach—and may use this in your work. You find it easy to let your mind "roam freely," and make good use of your imaginative powers. You probably feel enlivened by the chance

to work independently, but equally would enjoy "brainstorming" with others.

11-16: Negative. You probably have the idea fixed in your mind that you're not creative and therefore never give yourself the chance to find out. A fear of change and anything new and different may be restricting you from gaining more enjoyment from a new interest, or even from a routine task such as cooking, which can be highly creative. You might consider taking up a new hobby; for example, if you like working with your hands, you might consider sewing or pottery, or, if you prefer intellectual pursuits, you could join a reading group or take an evening class for which there are no exams. Let yourself go a little, and discover your creativity.

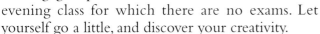

Pages 102–103:
Do You Overreact?

Mostly "a"s: You are probably the type of person everyone wants around in a crisis. You usually remain calm, and think of as many ways to respond as possible without getting flustered. You rarely act in haste, and are probably willing to listen to the advice of others before making a decision.

Mostly "b"s: Like most of us, your responses are erratic. You cope effectively most of the time: not brilliantly, perhaps, but not totally hopelessly either. By getting a clearer idea of your strengths and weaknesses, you will be able to cope more effectively.

Mostly "c"s: You have a tendency to overreact, and may express your feelings vehemently and excessively. You may, for example, become very irritable when things do not run smoothly, and express your anger and annoyance at the wrong time or take things out on the wrong people; or you may become weepy or distraught, making a mountain out of a molehill. Such overreactions often contribute to poor decisions.

Pages 112–113:
How Do You React?

Mostly "a"s: You respond almost entirely on the basis of your feelings, and you have a great deal of empathy for someone with a problem. While this makes you very supportive, you should guard against becoming too involved with someone else's crisis, which might lead you to neglect your own needs and responsibilities. You may also occasionally be too intrusive, particularly if the other person has made it clear he or she does not want any help.

Mostly "b"s: You recognize other people's feelings and are sympathetic, but may be embarrassed and unsure how to respond. This may make them feel awkward, too. Try reaching out to others more.

Mostly "c"s: You tend to use thinking and action, rather than feelings, to handle a crisis. This may be because you find feelings too painful, uncomfortable, or threatening to your need to remain in control, a response that may sometimes lead others to feel that you are insensitive.

Mostly "d"s: You find it difficult to handle strong emotions. You probably don't like it when other people show concern for you, and keep your distance from all but those to whom you feel closest and can trust.

Looking at your responses to the questions, you may find you chose a different type of response depending upon whether you felt close to the person involved. Not surprisingly, many people find it relatively easy—or at least want to try—to respond to someone close in a crisis, but find it harder with a comparative stranger. With close friends we have already established a degree of trust, rapport, and mutual support, whereas with strangers we feel unsure about how they may react.

INDEX

BIBLIOGRAPHY

Donna C. Aguilera, *Crisis Intervention: Theory & Method*; C. V. Mosby Co., St Louis, MO, U.S., 1970

Constance R. Ahrons, *The Good Divorce*; HarperCollins, New York, NY, U.S., 1994

Sheila Cane and Peter Lowman, *Putting Redundancy Behind You*; Kogan Page Ltd., London, U.K., 1993

Robert Dilts, *Changing Belief Systems with NLP*; Meta Publications, Cupertino, California, U.S., 1990

Dr. Windy Dryden, *10 Steps to Positive Living*; Sheldon Press, London, U.K., 1994

Peter Hildebrand, *Beyond Mid-Life Crisis: A Psychodynamic Approach to Ageing*; Sheldon Press, London, U.K., 1995

Sarah Litvinoff, *The Relate Guide to Better Relationships*; Vermilion, London, U.K., 1991

Sarah Litvinoff, *The Relate Guide to Starting Again*; Vermilion, London, U.K., 1993

Allan Mallinger and Jeanette De Wyze, *Too Perfect: When Being in Control Gets Out of Control*; Thorsons, HarperCollins, London, U.K., 1993

Ursula Markham, *Creating a Positive Self-Image: Simple Techniques to Transform Your Life*; Element Books Limited, Shaftesbury, Dorset, U.K., 1995

Stephen A. Murgatroyd and Ray D. Woolfe, *Coping with Crisis*; Harper & Row, London, U.K., 1982

Frank Parkinson, *Post-Trauma Stress*; Sheldon Press, London, U.K., 1993

Glenys Parry, *Coping With Crisis*; The British Psychological Society and Routledge Ltd., Leicester, U.K., 1990

Vera Peiffer, *Positively Fearless*; Element Books Limited, Shaftesbury, Dorset, U.K., 1993

Vera Peiffer, *Positive Thinking*; Element Books, Shaftesbury, Dorset, U.K., 1989

Vera Peiffer, *Strategies of Optimism*; Element Books Limited, Shaftesbury, Dorset, U.K., 1990

George Pollock and S. Greenspan, eds., *The Course of Life*; National Institute of Mental Health, Bethesda, MD, U.S., 1980 (George Pollock's essay "Ageing or Aged: Development or Pathology?")

Judith S. Wallerstein and Joan Kelly, *Surviving the Breakup: How Children and Parents Cope with Divorce*; HarperCollins, New York, NY, U.S., 1980

Anne N. Walther, *Divorce Hangover*; Mandarin, London, U.K., 1992

Paul Watzlawick, *The Situation is Hopeless, But Not Serious*; W.W. Norton & Co., New York, NY, U.S., 1983

Elizabeth Wilde McCormick, *Breakdown: Coping, Healing, and Rebuilding after Nervous Breakdown*; Unwin Hyman, London, 1988